augustine

The *Blackwell Great Minds* series gives readers a strong sense of the fundamental views of the great western philosophers and captures the relevance of these philosophers to the way we think and live today.

1. **Kant** by Allen W. Wood
2. **Augustine** by Gareth B. Matthews

Forthcoming
Aristotle by Jennifer Whiting
Descartes by Andre Gombay
Nietzsche by Richard Schacht
Plato by Paul Woodruff
Sartre by Katherine J. Morris
Spinoza by Don Garrett
Wittgenstein by Hans Sluga

blackwell great minds

edited by Steven Nadler

blackwell great minds

augustine

gareth b. matthews

© 2005 by Gareth B. Matthews

BLACKWELL PUBLISHING
350 Main Street, Malden, MA 02148-5020, USA
108 Cowley Road, Oxford OX4 1JF, UK
550 Swanston Street, Carlton, Victoria 3053, Australia

The right of Gareth B. Matthews to be identified as the Author of this Work has been asserted in accordance with the UK Copyright, Designs, and Patents Act 1988.

First published 2005 by Blackwell Publishing Ltd

Library of Congress Cataloging-in-Publication Data

Matthews, Gareth B., 1929–
    Augustine / Gareth B. Matthews.
        p. cm. — (Blackwell great minds)
    Includes bibliographical references and index.
    ISBN 0-631-23347-4 (alk. paper) — ISBN 0-631-23348-2 (pbk. : alk. paper)
1. Augustine, Saint, Bishop of Hippo.   I. Title.   II. Series.

    B655.Z7M18 2005
    189′.2—dc22
                                                              2004022247

A catalogue record for this title is available from the British Library.

Set in 9.5/12pt Trump Mediaeval
by Graphicraft Limited, Hong Kong
Printed and bound in the United Kingdom
by TJ International Ltd, Padstow, Cornwall

The publisher's policy is to use permanent paper from mills that operate a sustainable forestry policy, and which has been manufactured from pulp processed using acid-free and elementary chlorine-free practices. Furthermore, the publisher ensures that the text paper and cover board used have met acceptable environmental accreditation standards.

For further information on
Blackwell Publishing, visit our website:
www.blackwellpublishing.com

To
Richard Sorabji

contents

acknowledgments

I have used parts of "Augustine on reasoning from one's own case," *Medieval Philosophy and Theology* 7 (1998): 115–28, in chapter 7. I thank the editor for permission to do so.

Chapter 15 is a revised version of "Two concepts of happiness," which appeared in Jiyuan Yu and Jorge J. E. Gracia (eds.), *Rationality and Happiness: From the Ancients to the Early Medievals*. Rochester: University of Rochester Press, 2003, 161–74. I thank the editors and the University of Rochester Press for permission to use that material.

translations used

Translations in chapter 13 of passages from Plato's *Meno*, and in chapter 15 of Augustine, are my own. Unless otherwise attributed, passages from Augustine in other chapters are taken, sometimes with minor modifications, from the following translations:

Against the Academicians (*Contra academicos*), tr. Peter King. Indianapolis: Hackett, 1995.

City of God (*De civitate dei*), tr. Henry Bettenson. London: Penguin, 1984.

Confessions (*Confessiones*), tr. Henry Chadwick. Oxford: Oxford University Press, 1991.

Lying (*De mendacio*), tr. Sister Mary Sarah Muldowney, *Saint Augustine, Treatises on Various Subjects*. New York: Fathers of the Church, 1952, 16:46–110.

On Free Choice of the Will (*De libero arbitrio*), tr. Anna S. Benjamin and L. H. Hackstaff. Indianapolis: Bobbs-Merrill, 1964; also tr. Thomas Williams, Indianapolis: Hackett, 1993.

On the Immortality of the Soul (*De immortalitate animae*), tr. Ludwig Schopp, *Writings of Saint Augustine*. New York: Fathers of the Church, 1947, 2:3–55.

On the Trinity, ed. Gareth B. Matthews, tr. S. McKenna. Cambridge: Cambridge University Press, 2002.

The Teacher (*De magistro*), tr. Peter King. Indianapolis: Hackett, 1995.

Unfinished Literal Commentary on Genesis (*De genesi ad litteram imperfectus liber*), tr. Edmund Hill, *On Genesis*. Hyde Park, NY: New City Press, 2002, pp. 105–51.

References to Plato's *Republic* are from the translation by G. M. A. Grube, revised by C. D. C. Reeve. Indianapolis: Hackett, 1992.

References to Descartes are from *The Philosophical Writings of Descartes*, vols. 1 and 2, tr. J. Cottingham, R. Stoothoff, and D. Murdoch. Cambridge: Cambridge University Press, 1984–5. ("CSM, II, 53" will mean vol. 2, p. 53 of this translation. The additional AT citation will refer to the French text *Oeuvres de Descartes,* ed. C. Adam and P. Tannery. Paris: Vrin/CNRS, 1964–76. "At VII, 77" will mean vol. 7, p. 77 of this edition.)

Biblical passages are quotations from the Revised Standard Version, copyrighted 1946, 1952, © 1971, 1973, by the Division of Christian Education, National Council of the Churches of Christ in the USA.

the first-person point of view

The idea that the words 'I exist' (or their equivalent in Greek or Latin) might be used to state a philosophically important truth would have mystified the classical philosophers of antiquity. Of course it was important to each of them individually that they existed. Moreover, the existence of each of them individually was important to the development of philosophy. Without the existence of, say, Socrates, or Plato, or Aristotle, philosophy would not be what we know it to be today. But no major philosopher of antiquity would have thought of himself as expressing anything philosophically interesting by saying, "I exist."

This observation naturally leads to a second one. No philosopher of antiquity thought of doing philosophy from his own, singular point of view. That observation may come as a surprise. "What about the ancient relativists?" you might ask. Did they not suppose they had to start from how things seemed to them? And was not that doing philosophy from one's own, singular point of view?

The answer is 'No.' According to Plato, Protagoras, the most famous ancient relativist, said, "Each thing is to me such as it appears to me" (*Theaetetus* 152a). So far it might well *seem* that Protagoras is doing philosophy from his own first-person point of view. But we should note how the passage goes on. Protagoras adds, "and is to you such as it appears to you."

Protagoras's idea is that the wind is not, in itself, either hot or cold. The wind may be hot to me and cold to you; yet, in itself it is neither hot nor cold. Thus Protagoras denied that there is an objective fact about how things in the world are, independent of how they seem to be to this person or that. But his relativism was universal. He did not give any pride of place to how things seemed to *him*. Nor did he think he needed to start his philosophy by establishing how things seemed to him before he would be justified in allowing himself to suppose that there might be other points of view.

Protagoras does not explain how he knows there even exist other points of view. He just assumes that there are. He shows no special philosophical interest in other minds; he certainly does not suggest that one needs a philosophical argument to prove that they exist. And how things seemed to him in particular was not especially important to him. His point of view was, for him, just one among many, and not a privileged point of philosophical departure. His reflections were universal from the beginning, even if universally relativistic.

All this seems to have changed with Descartes. It was Descartes who first won broad acceptance for the suggestion that each of us must work out what we know individually, from our own first-person point of view, before we can move on to questions about how the world is, or might be, independently of us. And the foundation stone for the reconstruction of what it is we know, Descartes insisted, is the invulnerability of each philosopher's claim to know what we express when we say or think to ourselves, "I exist."

Much of modern philosophy and science has, of course, rejected this Cartesian starting point. But the Cartesian proposal has so fully insinuated itself into modern ways of thinking that it cannot be ignored, even if we would now like to do so. Popular culture, as well as academic philosophy, recognizes at least something of the significance of Cartesian first-personalism. Think of the very old *New Yorker* cartoon, in which a computer technician reads aloud, in perplexity, the output of a computer tape. "It says," he reports, "*cogito, ergo sum.*" Even the unphilosophical reader of the *New Yorker* will get the joke, and hence realize something of the significance of the philosophical problem of whether a computer could have a genuine thought from its own singular point of view. In fact, it may even cross that unphilosophical reader's mind that there is a question as to whether the computer literally has a point of view of its own.

Descartes does deserve the credit (or the blame!) for convincing much of the modern world that the first-person point of view must be taken seriously. Even, or perhaps I should say "especially," diehard critics of Descartes take him seriously. Of course, the appeal of the objectivist stance, that is, of making one's thought as nearly independent as possible from one's own personal perspective, is also very attractive to many thinkers. The goal of this sort of objectivism is to gain what Thomas Nagel has called, somewhat mischievously, "the view from nowhere."[1] Yet the suspicion that, in fact, the idea of a view from nowhere is really a myth, or at least a fiction, and that we delude ourselves if we do not each respect the philosophical priority of our own individual perspective, has not altogether lost its appeal. Moreover, for at least some among us, the sense that deferring to objectivism denudes knowledge of deep significance continues to be compelling.

So how did philosophers ever come to think that there is even a choice between beginning philosophy with an objectivist point of view and starting instead from a resolutely first-person point of view? Did Descartes himself simply make this idea up? Did his first-personalism emerge from out of nowhere? Certainly not. It began with Augustine.

Descartes himself denied that his thought had been influenced in any significant way by Augustine[2] – or by anyone else, for that matter! Scholars have debated whether that could possibly be true. A good way to appreciate its implausibility is to read Stephen Menn's intriguing book *Descartes and Augustine* (Cambridge: Cambridge University Press, 1998). My purpose here, however, is not to trace out Augustine's influence on Descartes. It is rather to introduce the philosophical thinking of the first thinker in Western philosophy actually to *do philosophy* from a genuinely first-person point of view.

There will, of course, be many references in my account of the philosophy of Augustine to Descartes, as well as to later modern thinkers, even to philosophers of the last century. But my treatment of Augustine is meant to be philosophy, not the history of ideas. To appreciate Augustine's originality one needs, of course, to have some conception of what went before him. And to appreciate its philosophical value we may need to make reference to what came after him. But it is the direct challenge of Augustine's own thinking that will be my primary focus in this book. I shall refer to philosophers who came before him and philosophers who came after primarily as a way of framing more clearly his own thought.

Throughout Augustine's corpus we find a striking appreciation for the philosophical importance of what each of us expresses by saying or thinking, "I exist." Thus, for example, in Book 2 of the dialogue *On Free Choice of the Will*, Augustine seeks to show how it can be made clear, and by 'made clear' he seems to mean 'proved,' that God exists. But as his starting point for that ambitious project he asks his interlocutor in the dialogue, Evodius, whether he, Evodius, exists. "Or are you, perhaps, afraid," he goes on, "that you are being deceived by my questioning?" Augustine adds, as if to reassure Evodius, "But if you did not exist, it would be impossible for you to be deceived" (2.3.7.20).

Augustine encourages Evodius to erect a number of conclusions on his unshakable conclusion that he himself exists. "Since it is clear to you that you exist, and since this would not be clear to you unless you lived," Augustine points out, "it is also clear to you that you are alive." He adds, "And this third point is also clear: you understand" (2.3.7.21). When Evodius agrees that these truths are clear to him, that is, have been proved to his satisfaction, Augustine lists the conclusions that Evodius has so far agreed to:

(1) I exist.
(2) I live.
(3) I understand that I exist and that I live.

On these three foundation stones, each certified by Evodius from his own first-personal point of view, Augustine invites him to reconstruct a skeletal account of the nature of the world, and eventually, a proof of the existence of God. Implicitly, Augustine invites readers of his dialogue to follow along and reconstruct their own account of the world, and, eventually, to accept their own proof of the existence of God. We shall return to Augustine's proof of the existence of God in chapter 10.

Other chapters to follow will bring out other philosophically interesting lines of reasoning in Augustine, most, although admittedly not all, of which are informed by a first-personal point of view in philosophy. Thus Augustine recognizes from this point of view what in modern philosophy is called "the problem of other minds" – the problem of how one can be assured that there are other minds in addition to one's own. So far as I know, he is the first philosopher to bring up this problem. Appropriately, Augustine also proposes a solution to the problem of other minds. His thinking on these matters will occupy chapter 7.

The account of time Augustine offers in Book 11 of his *Confessions*, perhaps his most widely admired contribution to philosophy today, is inconceivable apart from a thoroughly first-personal point of view. That topic will occupy us in chapter 9.

Augustine's account of the meanings of words in his dialogue *The Teacher*, and his thoughts about language acquisition in his *Confessions*, are both written from the speaker's or learner's point of view. His account of language acquisition, as we shall see, rests on an assumed recollection of what it was like for him as an infant to learn his first natural language. And his explanation of how we learn the meanings of new words aims to take seriously, in a philosophical way, the apparent limitation that each of us, as language learners, has no direct access to the mind of our teacher. We shall consider some of these issues in chapter 4.

The fact that we have dreams poses interestingly philosophical problems for Augustine. Thus he tries to respond to the old skeptical question "How do I know that I am not now dreaming?" More surprisingly, he also concerns himself with the question of what moral responsibility, if any, one bears for the actions of one's dream self. Augustine seems to be preoccupied especially with the sexual activity he has dreamt having. But the moral question about responsibility for the acts of one's dream self is, in fact, perfectly general. His concern could hardly arise for him in the way it does unless he considered himself actually *to be* his dream self, rather than a mere spectator of the dreams. He sees himself as isolated epistemologically from all other beings except God. These matters will be discussed in chapter 8.

Augustine offers several arguments for soul–body, or mind–body dualism. His most interesting argument for the dualism thesis rests, not on the difference between the idea of a mind and the idea of a body, as in Descartes, but rather on something else. His reasoning has to do with his conviction that nothing bodily need be present to a mind that is, nevertheless, fully present to itself. (See chapter 6.)

Augustine tells us that it was a work of Cicero's, now lost, that first turned him onto philosophy. Cicero not only awakened in Augustine the desire to seek philosophical wisdom; he also introduced him to philosophical skepticism. As we shall see in chapter 3, Augustine's response to skepticism itself takes a strikingly first-personal turn.

I have already pointed out reasoning in Augustine's *On Free Choice of the Will* that is remarkably similar to Descartes's "I think, therefore I am." Chapter 5 focuses on two additional passages in Augustine that display this same sort of reasoning. But, as we shall see, the role of such reasoning in Augustine is rather different from its role in Descartes.

It is not, however, just the philosophical problems Augustine recognizes, or the solutions he offers to those problems, that find their basis in his first-personal orientation. It is also the literary form of some of his most important works that takes this point of view. Thus his *Confessions*, which is the first important autobiography in Western literature, takes the literary form of an extended prayer to God. Since, as Augustine supposes, God already knows what is in the heart of the person praying and God never answers back, except in quoted verses of Scripture, the *Confessions* is actually a self-revelation that readers are allowed to, as it were, "overhear."

Augustine's *Soliloquies*, another work of great originality, takes the literary form of a dialogue. Yet the participants in this dialogue are not two different human beings, but rather Reason and the Soul. So, again, we have a work that reveals the self to the self. Interestingly, the Latin word *soliloquium* seems to have been coined by Augustine himself by putting together the Latin word for 'alone,' *solus,* and the word for 'speak,' *loquor.*

I do not mean to suggest that Augustine's only claim to philosophical distinction is his innovative resolve to do philosophy from his own singular point of view (with, of course, the implicit invitation to each of his readers to do the same thing, individually, for themselves). It is an exaggeration, but an excusable exaggeration, to say that Augustine was the father of modern philosophy of religion. Anyone who takes a course in the philosophy of religion in a college or university today can reasonably expect that the course, whatever else it covers, will at least take up these four topics: (1) Faith and Reason; (2) Arguments for the Existence of God;

(3) the Problem of Evil; and (4) the Problem of Divine Foreknowledge and Human Free Will. As we might expect, Augustine's discussion of each of these topics bears some important relation to the thought of some earlier philosopher. But Augustine's way of presenting and discussing these problems is so close to the way they get introduced in a modern course in the philosophy of religion that passages from his writings can easily be used in an introductory philosophy class today. I take up these topics in chapters 10, 11, and 12. I have included a chapter on Augustine on wanting bad things (chapter 13) to show how Augustine's view of the dark side of human motivation anticipates modern thinking and breaks with a tradition inaugurated by Socrates and Plato. I have included a chapter on Augustine on lying (chapter 14) to show how he initiates the philosophical discussion of the perplexities that plague any attempt to understand truthfulness, a topic largely neglected in classical Greek philosophy. Then there is a final chapter on Augustine on happiness (chapter 15), which, I hope, makes interesting connections both with Aristotle and with British empiricism.

Augustine is widely recognized as a great theological dogmatist. He delineated three important Christian heresies and in this way did as much as any single person to define Christian orthodoxy. He was therefore one of the greatest theological dogmatists of all time. At the same time he found some of the doctrines he defended, and the concepts in which they are expressed, philosophically perplexing. His sensitivity to philosophical perplexity makes his way of doing philosophy unmistakably Socratic. This Socratic side to his thinking is something I try to bring out as we go along.

Augustine is widely recognized to be a great theologian. That recognition is entirely appropriate. But Augustine is not so widely recognized today as an important philosopher. I hope this book will make a modest contribution toward correcting that imbalance.

further reading

Lynne Rudder Baker, "The first-person perspective: a test for naturalism," *American Philosophical Quarterly* 35 (1998): 327–48. This article offers a refreshing perspective on the importance of the first-person point of view in philosophy.

notes

1 Thomas Nagel, *The View from Nowhere* (New York: Oxford University Press, 1986).
2 See, e.g., his letter to Colvius, November 14, 1640, *The Philosophical Writings of Descartes*, tr. J. Cottingham, R. Stoothoff, D. Murdoch, and A. Kenny (Cambridge: Cambridge University Press, 1991), 2: 159–60.

augustine's life

A ugustine does not fit easily into our schemata for understanding the History of Western Philosophy. His dates, 354–430 CE, place him near the end of what we think of as ancient philosophy, during the period when the Hellenistic philosophies of Skepticism, Stoicism, and Neoplatonism dominated the philosophical scene. In fact, important Neoplatonic philosophers, such as Simplicius and Philoponous lived well into the second century after Augustine's death. So we might think that Augustine should be grouped with them.

Certainly Augustine was influenced by the main schools of Hellenistic philosophy. At more than one point in his life he was attracted to the skepticism of the New Academy. Stoicism also influenced his thinking, as scholars have recently come to emphasize. As for Neoplatonism, Augustine himself recognizes in his *Confessions*[1] the pivotal role "the books of the Platonists [i.e., Neoplatonists], translated from Greek into Latin" (7.9.13) played in his philosophical and religious development, even in his eventual conversion to Christianity.

Yet Augustine is not a Hellenistic philosopher. Instead, he is the first important Christian philosopher. He is also the first medieval philosopher, even though his life span does not belong to what we would otherwise think of as the Middle Ages. It belongs rather to what is best thought of as "late antiquity." In fact, if it were not for Augustine and Boethius (480–524), we would naturally think of medieval philosophy as beginning after the "dark ages," perhaps with John Scotus Eriugena (810–77), but more properly with Anselm of Canterbury (1033–1109), who was not born until six centuries after the death of Augustine!

Not only does Augustine fail to fit easily into the chronological categories in which we try to understand the history of Western philosophy, the place where he lived almost all his life is not one where we would expect to find any important philosophical thought at all. He was born in an inland town in North Africa, Thagaste, which is today Souk Ahras, in Algeria. Augustine did gain his higher education in Carthage, which is just north of modern Tunis, in Tunisia. But, except for a year in Rome

(383–4), and about six more years in Italy, mostly in Milan, he lived his whole life in North Africa.

Eventually Augustine became Bishop of Hippo Regius (near modern Bône, or Annaba, Algeria), which is a town on the coast of North Africa with a long history, but not a particularly memorable one. Hippo was quite a prosperous city in Augustine's day. But no other well-known figures, and certainly no other well-known philosophers or theologians, are associated with Hippo.

The anomaly of Augustine's placement in time and place is further complicated by the nature of his thought and its influence. John Rist has written an important book under the title *Augustine: Ancient Thought Baptized* (Cambridge: Cambridge University Press, 1994). What Rist's title suggests is that Augustine's philosophy is Christianized ancient philosophy. And there is certainly something appropriate about this characterization. What is missing from it, however, is the recognition that in Augustine philosophy also has a new beginning. The first-person point of view in philosophy I mentioned in the last chapter is not to be found in ancient philosophy. In fact, it is more important in modern philosophy, beginning with Descartes, than it is even in later medieval philosophy. Moreover, the ways in which Augustine departs from ancient philosophy are as important as the ways in which he draws on the philosophical tradition he inherits.

On the other hand, there are ways in which Augustine was very much a thinker of his own time and place. He was well educated in Latin literature and rhetoric. He was deeply involved in the theological controversies of his day, which, in fact he did more to shape than any other single person. He was caught up in the social and political turmoil of his time. Thus he addresses his great work *The City of God* to the question of whether the sack of Rome in 410 is a result of its conversion to Christianity. And the Vandal hordes approached Hippo in 430 as Augustine lay there on his deathbed.

Still, there are other ways in which Augustine does not belong at all to his time or place. His confessional style of writing, including his reflections on his own inner life, strikes us today as remarkably modern. As I have already pointed out, his *Confessions* is the first significant autobiography in Western literature. His remarkably Cartesian conception of mind, his way of framing the philosophical issues raised by mind, language, and religious belief prefigure what we think of today as modern thought. Oddly for a person whose life was spent mostly in a place otherwise unimportant to us, he is also a philosopher for our own time.

* * *

Augustine was the favored son of Monica, a devout Christian, and Patricius, a pagan until he was baptized on his deathbed. Augustine had a brother and sister, of whom we know almost nothing, and perhaps other siblings. It was Augustine on whom his family, and especially this mother, lavished their attention.

At age 12 Augustine was sent for secondary schooling to nearby Maudauros for 3 years. After returning to Thagaste for a year, Augustine went in 371 to Carthage for higher education. Augustine describes Carthage as a "cauldron of illicit loves" (3.1.1). No doubt it seemed a lecherous place to a small-town boy. In Carthage he soon found a mistress, who bore him a son, somewhat piously named "Adeodatus" ("given by God"). Augustine never tells us the name of his mistress, but he does claim to have been faithful to her (4.2.2).

To Augustine's great sorrow, Adeodatus died young, at age 18. We do not know exactly how important to his father Adeodatus was in his infancy or childhood. But Augustine's dialogue *The Teacher* is testimony to the probing philosophical conversations Augustine had with Adeodatus as a teenager.

Augustine's subject as a student at Carthage was rhetoric. He tells us that he was at the top of his class (3.3.6), and we can easily believe him. In fact, it is hard to imagine that any of his fellow students, or even his teachers, were nearly as astute or gifted as he. It was as a student in Carthage that Augustine discovered Cicero, who became his chief philosophical mentor. Augustine tells us that reading Cicero's *Hortensius*, a work that has not survived, changed his life by turning him to philosophy (3.4.7).

Cicero was not so much an original philosopher as an engaging presenter of the philosophical ideas of others. It was chiefly through Cicero that Augustine learned of the skepticism of the "New Academy," the successor to the Academy of Plato, and of the views of the Stoics and Epicureans.

At this time Augustine tried to read the Christian scriptures "to find out what they were like" (3.5.9). But he found the Bible "unworthy by comparison with the dignity of Cicero." Among the issues raised for him by this study of the Bible, no doubt the most significant one was "Where does evil come from?" (3.7.12). This issue dogged him throughout much of his life.

Consonant with his preoccupation with the origin of evil, Augustine became a Manichean "hearer" and remained one for nine years. The Manicheans, a Christian sect that flourished at the time, did at least offer a fairly clear response to the Problem of Evil. According to Manicheanism, there is a cosmic principle of darkness as well as a principle of light. What we experience in our lives is the warfare between the Kingdom of Light and the Kingdom of Darkness.

Augustine also faced a deep personal loss during this time of philosophical and religious searching. He devotes a long section of Book 4 of his *Confessions* to a description of the death of a close friend, whose name we are not given, and to the depression it caused in him. "My eyes looked for him everywhere," he writes, "and he was not there. I hated everything because they did not have him, nor could they tell me 'look, he is on the way', as used to be the case when he was alive and absent from me. I had become to myself a vast problem . . ." (4.4.9).

Augustine began his career as a teacher of rhetoric in Carthage in 376, at age 22. A few years later he wrote his first book, *On the Beautiful and the Fitting*, his copy of which he soon lost (3.13.20). The work did not survive.

When Augustine was 29, a famous Manichean bishop, Faustus, arrived in Carthage. Augustine tells us that he had waited nine years, the whole period of his Manichean apprenticeship, to put his questions about the Manichean faith to Bishop Faustus. But his encounter with the famous man turned out to be an utter disappointment to Augustine. "When I put forward some problems which troubled me," he writes in his *Confessions*, "I quickly discovered him to be ignorant of the liberal arts other than grammar and literature; and his knowledge was [only] of a conventional kind. He had read some orations of Cicero, a very few books by Seneca, some pieces of poetry, and some volumes of his own sect composed in a Latin of good style" (5.6.11).

But that was all – hardly enough to prepare him to deal with Augustine's probing questions. Augustine soon lost all hope that Faustus, or any other Manichean, could resolve the difficulties he had with the Manichean faith.

In 384 Augustine left Carthage to teach rhetoric in Rome. After only a year in Rome, a year plagued by illness, he moved to Milan, where he took up a teaching post under the city's new prefect. Ambrose was then Bishop of Milan and Augustine soon found himself listening to the sermons of Ambrose in the cathedral of Milan.

Ambrose became Augustine's mentor. In Ambrose Augustine finally found an intellectual peer. Ambrose had had a successful government career before his midlife conversion to Christianity. He was steeped in classical Greek learning and he was the first Latin Doctor of the Church. Augustine could not have known anyone like him in Carthage, let alone in Thagaste.

Augustine tells of how Ambrose received him like a father and with great kindness. He writes:

> I began to like him, at first indeed not as a teacher of the truth, for I had absolutely no confidence in your [i.e., God's] church, but as a human being who was kind to me. I used to listen enthusiastically to him preaching to the people, not with the intention which I ought to have had, but as if testing out his oratorical skill to see whether it merited the reputation it

enjoyed or whether his fluency was better than, or inferior to, what it was reported to be. I hung on his diction in rapt attention, but remained bored and contemptuous of the subject matter. My pleasure was in the charm of his language. (5.13.23)

But soon Augustine was won over to the content of Ambrose's sermons, as well as to the excellence of his oratory.

Augustine's disappointment with the Manichean Bishop Faustus had shaken his faith in Manicheanism. Faustus had shown himself incapable of dealing with Augustine's questions. Ambrose, by contrast, was a theologian of an entirely different order. It was he who led Augustine to make the crucial break with Manicheanism and to move away from the thought that, in desperation, he could always, like his mentor, Cicero, adopt the position of Academic skepticism. Augustine became a catechumen in the Catholic Church.

As Augustine describes this crucial turning point in his life, he gives special emphasis to its philosophical dimension. He writes:

I then energetically applied my critical faculty to see if there were decisive arguments by which I could somehow prove the Manichees wrong. If I had been able to conceive of spiritual substance, at once all their imagined inventions would have collapsed and my mind would have rejected them. But I could not. However, in regard to the physical world and all the natural order accessible to the bodily senses, consideration and comparison more and more convinced me that numerous philosophers held opinions much more probable than theirs. (5.14.25)

Augustine's mother, Monica, followed him to Milan. She, too, was attracted to Ambrose. And soon they were joined in Milan by friends from North Africa, including his patron, Romanianus, who had helped finance Augustine's higher education in Africa.

Gradually Augustine began to work his way out of the assumptions of philosophical materialism that Manicheanism had so long reinforced. At the same time he returned to the Problem of Evil, which he could no longer understand in the Manichean fashion as a consequence of the warfare between the Principle of Darkness and the Principle of Light. Either from Ambrose's sermons or from his own reading of Plotinus, which began in Milan, Augustine heard that "free choice of the will is the reason why we do wrong and suffer [God's] just judgment" (7.3.5). But, he says, he could not understand this idea. Augustine asked himself:

Who made me? Is not my God not only good but the supreme Good? Why then have I the power to will evil and to reject good? Is it to provide a reason why it is just for me to undergo punishments? ... If the devil was responsible, where did the devil come from? And if even he began as a good angel and became devil by a perversion of the will, how does the evil will by which he became devil originate in him, when an Angel is wholly made by a Creator who is pure goodness? (7.3.5)

Gradually Augustine worked his way through these issues and developed arguments against the Manichean position he had abandoned. He was helped in this by coming to read, in Latin translation, works by both Plotinus and his great pupil Porphyry. "By the Platonic books," he writes, "I was admonished to return into myself" (7.10.16). One result was what seems to have been his first mystical vision:

> With you [O God] as my guide I entered into my innermost citadel, and was given power to do so because you had become my helper. I entered and with my soul's eye, such as it was, saw above that same eye of my soul the immutable light higher than my mind – not the light of every day, obvious to anyone, nor a larger version of the same kind which would, as it were, have given out a much brighter light and filled everything with its magnitude. It was not that light, but a different thing, utterly different from all our kinds of light. (7.10.16)

Augustine became a Christian convert in July of 386, at the age of 32. Before he was baptized, he resigned his teaching position and retreated with his mother, his son, Adeodatus, then 15 years old, and a group of philosophically minded friends to a country estate, Cassiciacum, near Como. There he conducted philosophical conversations with these associates and wrote his earliest surviving work, *Against the Academicians*, as well as three other philosophical books.

At Easter of the next year, 387, Augustine and his son were baptized together in Milan cathedral. It was for Augustine a new beginning. "We were baptized," he writes in his *Confessions*, "and disquiet about our past life vanished from us" (9.6.14).

Together with Evodius, a fellow townsman from Thagaste, who was also to become a bishop and who is Augustine's interlocutor in his dialogue *On Free Choice of the Will*, Augustine resolved to form a Christian community in Africa. However, their return trip was halted at Ostia, the seaport of Rome, by a blockade. There Augustine's mother, Monica, fell ill. Realizing that Monica was near death, Augustine talked with her about the life the saints will have. He writes in his *Confessions*:

> The conversation led us towards the conclusion that the pleasure of the bodily senses, however delightful in the radiant light of this physical world, is seen by comparison with the life of eternity to be not even worth considering. Our minds were lifted up by an ardent affection towards eternal being itself. Step by step we climbed beyond all corporeal objects and the heaven itself, where sun, moon, and stars shed light on the earth.

We ascended even further by internal reflection and dialogue and wonder at your works, and we entered into our own minds. We moved up beyond them so as to attain to the region of inexhaustible abundance where you feed Israel eternally with truth for food. There life is the wisdom by which all creatures come into being, both things which were and will be. (9.10.24)

Augustine continues this description of the vision he shared with his mother for many more lines. It is, perhaps, his most eloquent description of a mystical vision.

After Augustine and his mother had concluded their vision together, Monica took her departure from him with this farewell speech: "My son, as for myself, I now find no pleasure in this life. What I have still to do here and why I am here, I do not know. My hope in this world is already fulfilled. The one reason why I wanted to stay longer in this life was my desire to see you a Catholic Christian before I die. My God has granted this in a way more than I had hoped" (9.10.26).

After nine days of illness, Monica died. She was 56. Augustine was 36.

Augustine and his associates, including his son, soon returned to Africa, indeed, to Thagaste, where they founded their Christian community. But in 391, while on a visit to Hippo, some 150 miles away, Augustine attended a service at the cathedral, where he was importuned by the assembled congregation to become a priest to assist the then Bishop of Hippo, Valerius. And so he was ordained. Five years later he himself became Bishop of Hippo.

Augustine founded a monastic community in Hippo, which became his own community for the rest of his life. His life as a bishop included pastoral duties, as well as a wide array of administrative responsibilities. He preached regularly. And he wrote, voluminously – sermons, letters, commentaries, and treatises. His literary output, produced with the help of scribes, is enormous. In addition to approximately 100 books and treatises there are approximately 250 letters and around 500 sermons, including those commenting on the Psalms.

Augustine devoted much of his energy and his writing to putting down what he viewed as important Christian heresies, especially Donatism, Manicheanism, and Pelagianism. In defining these heresies he thereby helped define Christian orthodoxy. A case could be made for saying that no theologian has ever done more to establish Christian orthodoxy than Augustine.

Two of the three heresies Augustine focused on, Pelagianism and Manicheanism, are of special philosophical interest. Pelagianism, so named for the British monk, Pelagius, who promulgated it, is epitomized in a maxim philosophers today associate with Immanuel Kant, namely, 'Ought implies can.' According to this view, if we have an obligation to be without sin, then it is within our power to be without sin. Augustine opposed Pelagianism with his insistence on the Doctrine of Original Sin, according to which, apart from the grace of God, none of us is capable of being without sin.

Manicheanism is the view that the cosmic force of evil is equal in power to the cosmic force of good. Although we should, of course, ally ourselves with the force of good, the principle of light, we can expect that the force of evil will continue to counterbalance goodness in the world.

In chapter 8 of this book we shall find a connection between Pelagianism and the Moral Dream Problem. And in chapter 12 we shall consider Manicheanism as one response to the Consistency Problem of Evil.

further reading

Peter Brown, *Augustine of Hippo*. Berkeley: University of California Press, 1967. This work has remained, ever since its publication, the standard biography of Augustine.

note

1 All quotations in this chapter are taken, unless otherwise noted, from Augustine's *Confessions*.

skepticism

Some people discover philosophy when they first begin to ask the grand questions, such as whether God exists, or whether we really have free will. Others discover philosophy when it first occurs to them that they may not even know for sure that they are now awake. Some people who first come to philosophy by asking grand questions later decide that they need to have an answer to skepticism about whether they have any knowledge at all before they can go on to consider issues about God and free will. Augustine seems to have followed this path.

When Augustine was 18 or 19 years old, he picked up and read a book by Cicero, *Hortensius*. That book, now lost, changed Augustine's life. As he reports in his *Confessions*, it kindled his love for philosophy and made him long for wisdom (3.4.7–8). In *On the Happy Life* he writes, "I was inflamed with so great a love for philosophy that I immediately thought of devoting myself to it" (1.4).

Augustine went on to read other works of Cicero. Some of them introduced him to philosophical skepticism. After that, there were times in his life when he toyed with the idea of becoming a philosophical skeptic himself. "The thought had come into my mind," he reports in Book 5 of his *Confessions*, that the philosophers whom they call "Academics" were shrewder than the others; they taught that everything is a matter of doubt, and that an understanding of the truth lies beyond human capacity (5.10.19).

Although the life of a philosophical skeptic seems not to have been an attractive option for very long periods in his life, Augustine continued to respond to the challenge of skepticism in all his major works.

Augustine's very earliest work, *On the Beautiful and the Fitting* (*De pulchro et apto*), has not survived. It seems to have been a work on aesthetics and the philosophy of mind in the grand tradition.[1] However, the earliest work of Augustine's that has survived, his *Against the Academicians*, is devoted entirely to the skepticism of the "New Academy," a school of philosophy founded by Arcesilaus (315–240 BCE) and carried on by Carneades (214–129/128 BCE). Augustine had been introduced to the views of these philosophers through Cicero's *Academica*.

Much of *Against the Academicians* is rather arcane and difficult to understand. But the third of the three books that make up the work becomes quite lively and philosophically fascinating. The project there is to determine whether anything can be known. The criterion for knowledge is something that gets called "Zeno's definition."[2] Unfortunately, Zeno's definition is stated in a number of different ways in the dialogue. The result is that the poor reader has a difficult time pinning down what Augustine takes it to be. The following quotation from Cicero's Academica (2.20.66) had already been stated in Book 2 of *Against the Academicians*:

T1. The truth that can be apprehended [*percipi*, perceived] is impressed on the mind by what it comes from in such a way that it couldn't be from something other than what it comes from. (2.5.11)

Here is one of Augustine's formulations of Zeno's definition in Book 3 of *Against the Academicians*:

T2. Zeno says that an appearance can be apprehended if it appears in such a way that it couldn't appear as a falsehood. (3.9.21)

Let's work with T2. A first thing to think about is the meaning of 'can be apprehended.' The Latin expression Augustine uses, *posse comprehendi*, suggests the translation 'can be grasped.' However, in the context, the main issue seems to be whether anything can be known. So let's just understand 'can be apprehended' to mean 'can be known.'

The second thing to think about is the meaning of 'appears in such a way that it couldn't appear as a falsehood.' This expression is meant to do the work of even more opaque expressions that Augustine uses in Book 2, such as 'is impressed on the mind by what it comes from in such a way that it couldn't be from something other than what it comes from.' That really daunting expression is, in fact, a direct quotation from Cicero's *Academica*, at 2.6.18. We should be grateful that we can work with T2 instead of Cicero's own formulation of Zeno's definition.

Even so, it is difficult to know what 'appears in such a way that it couldn't appear as a falsehood' means. Suppose I have the impression that there is a red rose in front of me right now. What would it be for the appearance of there being a red rose in front of me to "appear in such a way that it couldn't appear as a falsehood"? One might think it means that the appearance of the red rose in front of me could not appear as something illusory. I might be expected to say to myself when I have it,

"There is no way *that* could be an illusion." Then the idea would be that I can know that there is a red rose in front of me if, and only if, the appearance of there being a red rose in front of me does not seem in any way to be illusory. Yet that interpretation cannot be right. It makes the surrounding discussion implausible. Having knowledge of something cannot plausibly be construed as having an impression that does not *look* illusory.

I suggest that 'appears in such a way that it couldn't appear as a falsehood' must mean something like this: it appears in a way that something false cannot appear. I take the upshot to be that, when I really and truly know that p, it could not seem to me that p without its being, in fact, the case that p. A knowledge-guaranteeing impression that p, what the ancients called a "kataleptic" impression, is such that I cannot have that kind of impression that p without its being the case that p.

Interpreted in the way I am suggesting, and put schematically, Zeno's definition comes to the following:

(Z) A knows that p if, and only if, (i) it seems to A that p and
    (ii) it couldn't seem to A that p unless it were the case that p.

According to (Z) I pretty clearly do not know that there is a red rose in front of me. Thus, according to (Z), I know that there is a red rose in front of me, if, and only if, (i) it seems to me that there is a red rose in front of me and (ii) it could not seem to me that there is a red rose in front of me without there being a red rose in front of me. I suspect we can all agree that, no matter how vivid or colorful my impression of there being a red rose in front of me is, it is still possible that I am only under an illusion that there is a red rose in front of me. For one thing, I might be dreaming. Again, I might be hallucinating, perhaps from a dose of morphine or LSD. Or again, I might be in a virtual reality machine that produces the illusion in me of there being a red rose in front of me. So the second condition of (Z) is not satisfied and I do not know that there is a red rose in front of me.

The project of Book 3 of *Against the Academicians* is to see whether, given (Z), or something very much like it, there are other sorts of things that I do know.

Augustine looks, for his first candidate, to Zeno's definition itself. He asks, not whether we can know that the definition itself is true, but only – and this is a very clever move – whether we can at least know that Zeno's definition is *either true or false*. Here is the passage:

T3. Knowledge still doesn't abandon us, even if we are uncertain about [Zeno's definition]. We know that Zeno's definition is either true or false. Hence we do not know nothing. (3.9.21)

Augustine assumes here the Principle of Bivalence, that is, the principle according to which every statement is either true or false. Let us follow him in making that assumption. Most philosophers, until very recently, have been content to accept the Principle of Bivalence.

Assuming Bivalence, it seems that Augustine can know, according to (Z), that (Z) itself is either true or false. Thus, it can certainly seem to him that (Z) is either true or false; so condition (i) of (Z) is satisfied. Moreover, it cannot seem to him to be true or false unless it is true or false – for the very good reason that it cannot fail to be one or the other anyway. So Augustine can claim, and, in fact, does claim, to know something.

One might think that this application of (Z) to the statement, '(Z) is either true or false' is a cheat. These impressions that Zeno himself had in mind are supposed to be "kataleptic," that is, self-guaranteeing by the way they are received and, for this reason, to reflect accurately what they are impressions of. What is there about the way the impression that some statement, S, is either true or false that guarantees that it reflects correctly what it is the impression of? Is not what guarantees that the impression that 'S is either true or false' could not be false simply the fact that 'S is either true or false' is a logical truth and therefore could not be false? Thus, however poorly or inappropriately the impression that 'S is either true or false' is received, the statement itself simply could not be false.

Perhaps what Augustine should say is that any *correct* impression of a logical truth will be guaranteed to be true. I am unsure whether that is cheating on Zeno or not. But at least it does seem to make sense of Augustine's counterexample. In any case, where the proposition that p states a necessary truth, it cannot seem to me to be the case that p without its being the case that p.

Augustine's next example of something he claims to know is somewhat tricky to interpret. Here is the next important passage in *Against the Academicians*, Book 3:

> T4. Although I'm still far from being anywhere close to a wise man, I do know some things in physics. I'm certain that the world is either one [in number] or not – and, if there isn't just one world, the number of worlds is either finite or infinite . . .
>
> Similarly, I know that this world of ours has been arranged as it is either by the nature of bodies or by some providence; that it always was and will be, or began to be and is never going to end, or did not have a beginning in time but is going to have an end, or it began to exist in time and is not going to exist forever. (3.10.23)

No doubt Augustine is hoping that

(1) The world is either one [in number] or not

will count as a necessary truth in much the way his previous example

(2) Zeno's definition is either true or false

does. But on a standard way of understanding of (1), it entails

(3) There is a world

which is not a necessary truth. (1) entails (3) because of the definite article in front of 'world.' Since (1) entails (3) and (3) is not a necessary truth, (1) is not a necessary truth either.

However, before we reject this putative example of something we can know, we should note that there is no definite article in Augustine's Latin (*certum enim habeo aut unum esse mundum aut non unum*). We can therefore read him as making this claim:

(4) Either there is one world or there is not one world

which does, I think, count as a logical truth.

So far Augustine seems to have refuted global skepticism by producing two examples of things that we can know. The next suggestion in T4 is less troublesome:

(5) If there isn't just one world, the number of worlds is either finite or infinite

We can easily understand (5) to mean this:

(6) If there is more than one world, then the number of worlds is either finite or infinite.

And (6) does indeed look like a necessary truth. And so, according to (Z), it, too, can be known.

After T4 we come to a most fascinating passage. The Academic skeptic offers Augustine the following challenge:

> T5. How do you know that the world [even] exists, . . . if the senses are deceptive? (3.11.24)

This is perhaps the most remarkable skeptical challenge in the whole treatise. It introduces what, in modern philosophy, is called "the Problem of the External World." Augustine's response is equally remarkable:

> T6. Therefore, I call the whole that contains and sustains us, whatever it is, "the world," – the whole, I say, that appears before my eyes, which I

perceive to include the heavens and the earth (or the quasi-heavens and quasi-earth). . . .

You'll ask me, "Is what you see the world even if you're asleep?"

It has already been said that I call "the world" whatever seems to me to be such. (3.11.24–5)

Augustine is introducing here, perhaps for the first time in Western philosophy, the idea of one's own phenomenal world, the world of appearances that one is aware of as a conscious subject, or mind. The idea of a phenomenal world is generally thought to be a modern idea, original with Descartes. But here it is in Augustine.

Augustine does not develop this idea any further. He never poses the Problem of the External World, as Descartes does in this famous passage:

. . . every sensory experience I have ever thought I was having while awake I can also think of myself as sometimes having while asleep; and since I do not believe that what I seem to perceive in sleep comes from things located outside me, I did not see that I should be any more inclined to believe this of what I think I perceive while awake. (Descartes, *Meditation* VI, AT VII, 77; CSM, II, 53)

Still, what Augustine does say in *Against the Academicians*, Book 3, invites Descartes's problem.

Augustine goes on to consider some other mathematical truths as examples of things we can know:

T7. . . . if there is one world and [there are six] worlds, then, whatever condition I may be in, it's clear that there are seven worlds, and it isn't presumptuous of me to affirm that I know this.

Accordingly, prove that either this inference or those disjunctions given above can be false because of sleep, madness, or the unreliability of the senses! . . . For that three times three is nine and [is] the square of rational numbers must be true, even if the human race be snoring away! (3.11.25)

The last set of examples is also quite fascinating. They are cases of knowing how things *seem* to us:

T8. Don't assent to more than that you're convinced it appears so to you, and then there isn't any deception. I don't see how even an Academician can refute someone who says: "I know that this seems white to me; I know that this sound is pleasant to me; I know that this smells good to me; I know that this tastes sweet to me; I know that this seems cold to me."

"Tell me instead whether the leaves of the wild olive tree, which the goat so stubbornly desires, are bitter in themselves."

"You shameless man! The goat itself has more modesty! I don't know how they are to brute animals, but they are bitter to me. What more do you ask?" (3.11.26)

The upshot of *Against the Academicians*, Book 3, is this. Even if I am dreaming, there are many things I can know. Specifically, I can know (1) logical truths; (2) mathematical truths; (3) the existence of my own phenomenal world; and (4) how things seem to me.

We might pause to note that the items in the first two categories can qualify as knowledge according to (Z) chiefly by being necessary truths. Thus its seeming to me that $7 + 5 = 12$ becomes knowledge by the fact that what seems to me to be the case is, in fact, necessarily the case. It is not that my impressions of mathematical truths, just as impressions, have any knowledge-guaranteeing quality about them. It is rather that, say, '$7 + 5 = 12$' has a special self-guaranteeing quality by expressing a necessary truth.

The items in categories (3) and (4) are quite different. Unlike '$7 + 5 = 12$,' 'It seems to me that there is a world out there' is not a necessary truth.' Nor is 'That tastes bitter to me.' These impressions are self-certifying, or self-guaranteeing, impressions in the sense that, if I have such an impression, I know I have it.

Augustine, in his later writings, shows little interest in (4). He remains interested in (1) and (2), the truths of logic and mathematics, which count for him as Eternal Truths that can be grasped directly by the human mind. They are among the "intelligible things" Augustine refers to in this passage from his late treatise, *On the Trinity*:

T9. . . . the nature of the intellectual mind is so formed as to see those things which, according to the disposition of the Creator, are subjoined to intelligible things in the natural order, in a sort of incorporeal light of its own kind, as the eye of the flesh sees the things that lie about it in this corporeal light, of which light it is made to be receptive and to which it is adapted. (12.15.24)

Augustine's interest in (3) the phenomenal world each of us can know we have, becomes, in his later writing, an interest in the mind and what it can know about itself. That interest is prefigured in this important passage from near the end of *Against the Academicians*, in which Augustine first speaks of what the human mind or soul can know of itself:

T10. . . . Plato perceived that there are two worlds: an intelligible world where truth itself resides, and this sensible world that we obviously sense by sight and touch. The former is the true world, the latter only truthlike and made to its image. Consequently, truth about the former world is refined and brightened, so to speak, in the soul that knows itself, whereas only opinion and not knowledge, can be engendered about the latter world . . . (3.17.37)

Although Augustine does not make the point in *Against the Academicians*, he comes later to insist that the "inner knowledge" that each of us has of ourselves includes what each of us expresses by saying or thinking, "I exist." As we shall see in chapter 5, the knowledge each of us has of our own existence becomes Augustine's most arresting and most potent response to the challenge of Academic skepticism. Moreover, the "inner knowledge" each of us has of ourselves forms the basis, as we shall see in chapter 6, of Augustine's reasoning for mind–body dualism.

further reading

Christopher Kirwan, *Augustine*. London: Routledge, 1989, ch. 2, "Against the sceptics." This chapter offers a close analysis and assessment of Augustine's reasoning in *Against the Academicians*.

notes

1 See *Confessions* 4.14.23–15.24.
2 Zeno of Citium (ca. 334–262 BCE), not the Zeno of Zeno's paradoxes.

language

As we saw in the chapter 3, Augustine does not really take the idea of solipsism seriously. He claims in *Against the Academicians* that, if I call "the world" what appears to me to be the world, then I can know that the world exists. But his saying that is only part of his ongoing effort to show that, contrary to Academic skepticism, there are at least some things that can be known. Augustine does not attempt to ask, in the fashion of Descartes, whether, and if so, how, I can know that, in addition to my phenomenal world, there is a physical world that exists independently of me and my impressions of such a world. Put in the jargon of twentieth-century philosophy, he does not recognize the Problem of the External World, let alone try to solve it.

There is a way, however, in which Augustine does take ego isolation very seriously. He imagines how it was for him as an infant, before he had learned the words of any natural language. He tells us how he tried to understand the world about him and to communicate his thoughts and desires to others. The following passage from Book 1 of his *Confessions* presents a vivid picture of social and epistemological isolation in the midst of caring adults:

> T1. Little by little I began to be aware where I was and wanted to manifest my wishes to those who could fulfil them as I could not. For my desires were internal; adults were external to me and had no means of entering into my soul. So I threw my limbs about and uttered sounds, signs resembling my wishes, the small number of signs of which I was capable but such signs as lay in my power to use: for there was no real resemblance. When I did not get my way, either because I was not understood or lest it be harmful to me, I used to be indignant with my seniors for their disobedience, and with free people who were not slaves to my interests; and I would revenge myself upon them by weeping. That this is the way of infants I have learnt from those I have been able to watch. That is what I was like myself and . . . they have taught me more than my nurses with all their knowledge of how I behaved. (1.6.8)

Several things about this passage are especially fascinating. One thing is the assumption that infant Augustine had a quite fully developed capacity to think and reason long before he had acquired a public language in which to express his thoughts and desires. Another thing is the suggestion, first made and then later retracted, that the nonlinguistic signs he made to those around him who could fulfill his wishes actually resembled his wishes. What could it be to make a sign that resembles one's wish?

Perhaps what Augustine means in this passage is that he made signs resembling the fulfillment of his wishes. Thus he might have pursed his lips and made a sucking sound to imitate the act of sucking milk from his mother's breast. If he had done that to indicate his desire for milk, the sign could be said to resemble the fulfillment of his desire for sucking at his mother's breast.

Yet infants also cry when they suffer gastric distress. What sign could one make that would resemble the wish to be relieved of gastric distress? I must say that I have no idea.

It was certainly natural to suppose that gestures are understood because they resemble in some way what one wishes for. But Augustine was also right to withdraw the suggestion that resemblance is a universal key to understanding, from the behavior of an infant, what that infant wants. It seems that there is in fact no single, universal key to understanding that.

Long before an infant comes to be able to use the words of a natural language such as Latin (or perhaps for infant Augustine, Punic) to communicate with others, that infant will have developed the capacity to make known a number of different wishes. But how does an infant make the transition from gesture to real language? Here is part of Augustine's account of that transition. It is a passage from the *Confessions* that Wittgenstein uses as the opening for his great work the *Philosophical Investigations*:

> T2. When they (my elders) named some object, and accordingly moved towards something, I saw this and I grasped that the thing was called by the sound they uttered when they meant to point it out. Their intention was shown by their bodily movements, as it were the natural language of all peoples: the expression of the face, the play of the eyes, the movement of other parts of the body, and the tone of voice which expresses our state of mind in seeking, having, rejecting, or avoiding something. Thus, as I heard words repeatedly used in their proper places in various sentences, I gradually learnt to understand what objects they signified; and after I had trained my mouth to form these signs, I used them to express my own desires.[1]

Wittgenstein uses this quotation to identify a conception of language he wants to discuss and criticize in his *Philosophical Investigations*. Wittgenstein seems to have thought he found expressed in T2 a very important, but quite mistaken, view of the nature of language. This mistaken view is what G. P. Baker and P. M. S. Hacker, in their influential commentary, have called "Augustine's picture of language" – a picture that Wittgenstein seems to link with Gottlob Frege (1848–1925), Bertrand Russell (1872–1970), and perhaps especially with his own early work, the *Tractatus*. The Augustinian picture of language as it emerges in the *Philosophical Investigations* is thus, it seems, primarily a target for presenting, assessing, and criticizing views on the nature of language prominent in the first half of the twentieth century, even though the philosophers who made those views prominent, including Wittgenstein himself, when he wrote the *Tractatus*, did not think of themselves as Augustinians.

Among the rather large number of theses that Baker and Hacker identify in Wittgenstein's "Augustinian picture of language" are these:

(i) Any significant word signifies something. Its meaning is what it stands for or signifies. It is assigned a meaning by correlating it with an object. Such a correlation gives it a meaning by making it into a name of an object. It represents the object it stands for. . . .

(ii) . . . Since verbal definitions merely explain one expression by means of others and hence constitute connections within language, ostensive definitions provide the only possible means for correlating words with things . . .

(iii) The thesis that all words are names is equivalent to the thesis that the fundamental form of explanation of words is ostensive definition, that ostensive definitions are the foundation of language. . . .[2]

According to this "Augustinian picture of language" each of us breaks out of our epistemological ego isolation by having the names of things pointed out to us in such a way that we come to be able to express our own desires by using the words we have learned by ostensive definition. Thus 'Milk!' can express a desire for milk, and 'Banana!' a desire for some banana.

In fact, this conception of language learning does not square well with what we find in Augustine's early dialogue *The Teacher*, which is Augustine's most inviting presentation of his philosophy of language. As I mentioned in chapter 2, *The Teacher* is a dialogue between Augustine and his son, Adeodatus. Augustine says this about it in his *Confessions*:

T3. One of my books is entitled *The Teacher*. There Adeodatus is in dialogue with me. You [O, God,] know that he was responsible for all the ideas there attributed to him in the role of my partner in the conversation. He was 16 at the time. I learnt many other remarkable things about him. His intelligence left me awestruck. Who but you could be the maker of such wonders? (9.6.14)

In fact, Adeodatus does make some very astute points in the dialogue.

The dialogue begins with Augustine's question 'What do we want to accomplish when we speak?' Adeodatus replies with this thesis:

(A1) When we speak, we want either to teach or to learn. (1.1)

Augustine tries to bring that disjunctive purpose under a single purpose. Suggesting that, when we want to learn something, we are teaching our conversation party what we want to learn, Augustine gets Adeodatus to agree that (A1) can be reduced to this:

(A2) When we speak we want to teach someone something. (1.1)

Adeodatus now comes up with a clever counterexample to (A2), namely, singing: "Given that we often sing while we're alone, without anyone [else] present who might learn," he points out, "I don't think we want to teach anything."

Augustine's response to Adeodatus's well-targeted counterexample is, one has to admit, somewhat lame. Augustine points out that we sometimes teach by reminding someone of something. He suggests that when we sing we teach ourselves by reminding ourselves of something we already know.

Adeodatus, however, stands his ground. "I would seldom sing to remind myself," he replies; "I do it only to please myself." Score a point for Adeodatus!

Using what looks like nothing more than a bit of sophistry, Augustine gets Adeodatus to agree to this new thesis:

(A3) When we speak we want to teach or remind someone of something. (1.2)

Adeodatus now comes up with another telling counterexample: prayer. "We certainly speak while we're praying, and yet it isn't right to believe that we teach God or remind Him of anything" (1.2).

Augustine replies with a little sermon on what is supposed to happen in prayer. It is not clear to me that he succeeds in neutralizing Adeodatus's counterexample. But Adeodatus here plays the role of the good son and drops his opposition.

This opening section of the dialogue also contains some interesting points I have left out. But, to me, the most instructive thing about it is the way Augustine, like most philosophers, insists on trying to state the purpose of using language in one simple thesis. Wisely, Adeodatus resists the pressure from his father to simplify. His sensitivity to the variety of things we do with words might remind a philosopher today of Ludwig Wittgenstein's *Philosophical Investigations* or J. L. Austin's *How To Do Things With Words.*

Philosophers then and now are much too quick to assume that the point of using language is always the same thing, namely, the transfer of information. According to this picture, the speaker is always passing on information to the hearer, or else soliciting information from the hearer. Part of the reason Wittgenstein talks about what he calls "language-games" is to remind us of the variety of ways in which words are used and the variety of contexts in which we use them. Here is a famous passage from the *Philosophical Investigations*, which makes that point:

T4. Review the multiplicity of Language-games in the following examples, and in others:

Giving orders, and obeying them –
Describing the appearance of an object, or giving its measurements –
Reporting an event –
Speculating about an event –
Forming and testing a hypothesis –
Presenting the results of an experiment in tables and diagrams –
Making up a story; and reading it –
Play-acting –
Singing catches –
Guessing riddles –
Making a joke; telling it –
Solving a problem in practical arithmetic –
Translating from one language into another –
Asking, thanking, cursing, greeting, praying.[3]

It is ironical that, in his dialogue *The Teacher* Augustine has his own son, Adeodatus, resist what Baker and Hacker call the "Augustinian picture of language." Augustine's tribute to his son is also a tribute to his own appreciation of the points his son makes in the dialogue.

The dialogue soon moves on to a consideration of the meanings of words. Words, Augustine says, are signs, and a sign cannot be a sign, he insists, unless it signifies something (2.3). So this is the thesis Augustine proposes:

(A4) Every word is a sign and every sign signifies something.

Augustine tests (A4) with a line from Virgil's *Aeneid*, which begins this way:

If nothing from so great a city . . .

The first word in that line is already a challenge for (A4). Augustine presses Adeodatus to say what the word 'if' (Latin: *si*) signifies. After some hesitation Adeodatus replies that it signifies doubt.

Augustine than asks Adeodatus what 'nothing' (Latin: *nihil*) signifies. His son replies, "That which doesn't exist." The question of what 'nothing' means, or signifies, is, of course, a very tricky one. Augustine understands Adeodatus's reply to commit him to the conclusion that the word 'nothing' signifies nothing. Of course, if 'nothing' did signify nothing, we could reasonably conclude that the word is meaningless, which would be absurd.

However, it is not at all obvious that Adeodatus's reply ('That which doesn't exist') commits him to this conclusion that 'nothing' is without signification. Augustine would have been better served to point out that substituting 'that which doesn't exist' for 'nothing' in a sentence, for example, in this one,

(a) Nothing is better than a cold beer on a hot day

would yield

(b) That which doesn't exist is better than a cold beer on a hot day.

Which is hardly what we want.

Clearly (a) and (b) do not mean the same thing. So 'nothing' in (a) does not mean 'that which does not exist.'

In any case, Augustine himself suggests that 'nothing,' like 'if,' signifies a state of mind. Whereas the state of mind signified by 'if' was said to be doubt, the state of mind signified by 'nothing' is said to be the frustrated state of having looked around for something and finding that what one was looking for does not exist. But clearly 'I have looked around and found that what I was looking for does not exist' cannot be substituted for occurrences of 'nothing' in such a way as to preserve meaning either.

Later medieval philosophers called words such as 'if' and 'nothing' "syncategorematic terms." Their idea was that such words do not signify anything by themselves, but only in conjunction with other terms. Their meaning must be given by specifying the syntactic role they play in the statements in which they appear.

The difficulty Augustine and his son have in saying what 'if' and 'nothing' signify reveals that these terms need to be understood in a rather different way from the way "categorematic" terms such as 'man,' 'horse,' and 'tree' are understood. But neither Augustine nor his son offers a satisfactory diagnosis of this difference. Faced with a perplexity about what 'if' and 'nothing' could possibly be thought to signify, they turn away from the question of what the words themselves signify to a question about what might be the significance of someone's *uttering* them.

Suppose you ask me where my daughter is and I reply, "She is either in the family room or in the kitchen." My saying that in response to your question might well be taken, in normal circumstances, to express an uncertainty about where my daughter is. But we should hardly conclude from that that the word 'or' itself signifies uncertainty.

Lest we be too hard on Augustine, however, it might be worth pointing out that no less a philosopher than Bertrand Russell once made a similar move. He writes:

> In logic, "p" implies "p or q," but in psychology the state of mind of a person asserting "p" is different from that of a person asserting "p or q," unless the person concerned is a logician. Suppose I am asked, "What day was it you went to London?" ... If I know it was Tuesday, I shall not reply, "Tuesday or Wednesday," in spite of the fact that this answer would be true. In fact we only use the word "or" when we are uncertain, and if we were omniscient, we could express our knowledge without the use of this word – except, indeed, our knowledge as to the state of mind of those aware of a greater or lesser degree of ignorance.[4]

Russell's point falls into line with the idea of "conversational implicature," developed by Paul Grice.[5] According to Grice, it is a maxim of conversation that one give as much information as required. Thus, if I believe that my daughter is in the kitchen, rather than in the living room, I will be violating a conversational implicature to say that she is either in the one or the other, even though, of course, the disjunctive claim will also be true, provided either disjunct is true. In any case, Russell, like Augustine, seems to have focused on the meaning of someone's saying "... or ..." rather than on the meaning of 'or' itself. Those two kinds of meaning need to be kept distinct.

The discussion in *The Teacher* then turns to questions about whether what a word signifies can be shown by pointing. This is the issue of ostensive learning we connected earlier in the chapter with Baker and Hacker's commentary on Wittgenstein, and with T2, Augustine's own account in his *Confessions* of how he learned the meanings of words from the adults around him. Conceived as a question about how we can, as infants, break out of our ego isolation by learning a language, it asks whether adults can use pointing and showing to enable infants to connect words to persons, objects, and events in the world.

Ostensive learning, as Augustine discusses it with Adeodatus, includes not only pointing with a finger to the object signified, but also demonstrating or showing something without a sign. In the *Teacher* Augustine's most instructive example is 'walking.' Augustine wants to know from

Adeodatus how one who is already engaged in walking can, while walking, show another what 'walking' signifies. Adeodatus replies that one could walk a little faster (3.5). Devastatingly, Augustine asks Adeodatus if he does not realize that hurrying is something different from walking.

Later on, Adeodatus embellishes Augustine's point:

> T5. . . . how shall I guard against his thinking that it's just the amount of walking I have done? He'll be mistaken if he thinks this. He'll think that anyone who walks farther than I have, or not as far, hasn't walked at all. (10.29)

The walking example becomes emblematic in the *Teacher* for the ambiguity of ostension. Certainly walking is different from hurrying. Walking is also different from, say, pacing, taking 55 steps, sauntering, and a host of other things that the demonstrator might be taken to have demonstrated. Ostensive learning is, it seems, chronically and unavoidably plagued with such ambiguity. So how can language learning ever be successful if, as Baker and Hacker characterize the "Augustinian picture of language," "ostensive definitions provide[s] the only possible means for correlating words with things."[6] And how could Augustine be right when he states in T2, "When they (my elders) named some object, and accordingly moved towards something, I saw this and I grasped that the thing was called by the sound they uttered when they meant to point it out"?

Myles Burnyeat pointed out some time ago (see "Suggested additional reading" below) that T2, the quotation with which Wittgenstein begins his *Philosophical Investigations*, omits important prefatory remarks that come earlier in that paragraph. Those remarks are crucial for understanding Augustine's position on ostensive learning. These two sentences are especially important:

> T6. It was not that grown-up people instructed me by presenting me with words in a certain order by formal teaching, as I was to learn the letters of the alphabet. I myself acquired this power of speech with the intelligence which you gave me, my God. (1.8.13)

So it is not, after all, Augustine's idea that his elders set up unambiguous ostensive learning situations for him. Rather it is his claim that his own intelligence enabled him to figure out the reference of the words spoken in his presence. And this, it turns out, is the solution to the problem of the ambiguity of ostension that Augustine presents in the *Teacher*. Here is the crucial passage:

> T7. Augustine: . . . Consider this example. Suppose that someone unfamiliar with how to trick birds (which is done with reeds and birdlime) should

run into a birdcatcher outfitted with his tools, not birdcatching but on his way to do so. On seeing this birdcatcher, he follows closely in his footsteps, and, as it happens, he reflects and asks himself in his astonishment what exactly the man's equipment means. Now the birdcatcher, wanting to show off after seeing the attention focused on him, prepares his reeds and with his birdcall and his hawk intercepts, subdues, and captures some little bird he has noticed nearby. I ask you, wouldn't he then teach the man watching him what he wanted to know by the thing itself rather than by anything that signifies [e.g., by words]?

Adeodatus: I'm afraid that everything here is like what I said about the man who asks what it is to walk . . .

Augustine: It's easy to get rid of your worry. I add that he's so intelligent that he recognizes the kind of craft as a whole on the basis of what he has seen . . .

Adeodatus: I also can add this to the other case! If he is sufficiently intelligent, he'll know the whole of what it is to walk, once walking has been illustrated by a few steps.

Augustine: You may do so as far as I'm concerned . . . (10.32)

So it is God-given intelligence that enables us to learn from ostension, not simply the juxtaposition of sign and object signified. Without that intelligence, the chronic ambiguity of ostension would block learning.

At the end of the *Teacher* Augustine puts this point in theological terms. With respect to all of the things we understand, Augustine says we consult "not the speaker who makes a noise outside us – but the Truth that presides over the mind within" (11.38). The Truth is then identified as Christ, the Teacher. "The sun, . . . the moon and the other stars, the lands and the seas, and all things which are generated in them without number," Augustine writes, "are all exhibited and shown through themselves by God and nature to those who perceive them" (10.32).

Thus the account of language learning in Book 1 of the *Confessions* seems not to be at odds with Augustine's insistence, in *The Teacher*, that ostensive teaching is always ambiguous. If it were not for our God-given intelligence and the illumination provided by the Inner Teacher, we would never learn what 'wall' or 'walking' or 'bird-catching' means.

Of course, Augustine's Doctrine of Illumination would be no more welcome to Wittgenstein than the picture of learning through ostension that he attributes to Augustine. But it is important to realize that Augustine was himself well aware of the ambiguity of ostension.

Does the Doctrine of Illumination have any appeal to any philosophers or linguists today? Consider this explanation by Jerrold Katz of the view he calls "linguistic rationalism," a view which he himself defends:

Linguistic rationalism claims that all the concepts available to science and everyday explanation are contained in the innate space of possible senses with which humans face the task of language acquisition. The notion of innate space of possible senses is to be understood in the context of Chomsky's now familiar Cartesian position on language acquisition. Chomsky argues that only a theory of acquisition that posits innate grammatical principles rich enough to specify the set of all possible grammars can account for the fact that normal children learn the immensely complex structures of a natural language quickly, uniformly, and on the basis of highly degraded samples of speech. On our view, the posit of such innate grammatical principles includes semantic principles that specify the space of possible senses.[7]

Katz views the senses of words compositionally, in such a way that if, for example, *motion, by means of, two,* and *legs* were semantic simples, they could be put together logically to form the complex concept *walking*. If, then, as Katz supposes, each of us normal human beings has innately available to us the space of all possible senses, the light of Divine illumination might lead us to pick out these simples, combine them in the right way, and come up with the concept of walking.

Other innatists among the theorists of language acquisition may or may not find Katz's linguistic rationalism attractive. They may have a different story to tell. My point is that some good theorists of language acquisition are innatists. And innatist theories can usually be framed in Augustinian terms, provided that reference to Christ, the Inner Teacher, is stripped of its explicitly theological meaning. In this way it is not too much of a stretch to say that Augustinianism lives on today in theories of language learning, though garbed now in fully secular clothes, and made more sophisticated by, among other things, distinguishing carefully between categorematic terms and syncategorematic terms.

further reading

M. F. Burnyeat, "Wittgenstein and Augustine *De magistro*," reprinted in Gareth B. Matthews (ed.), *The Augustinian Tradition*. Berkeley: University of California Press, 1999, pp. 286–303. Burnyeat corrects the impression Wittgenstein gives us concerning Augustine's views about ostension in language learning.

notes

1 *Philosophical Investigations*, 2nd edition, tr. G. E. M. Anscombe (Oxford: Basil Blackwell, 1967).
2 G. P. Baker and P. M. S. Hacker, *Wittgenstein: Understanding and Meaning* (Oxford: Basil Blackwell, 1980), pp. 36–7.
3 Wittgenstein, *Philosophical Investigations*, pt. I, ¶23.
4 *Human Knowledge: Its Scope and Limits* (New York: Simon & Schuster, 1948), p. 127.

5 See his *Studies in the Way of Words* (Cambridge, MA: Harvard University Press, 1989).
6 Baker and Hacker, *Wittgenstein*, p. 36.
7 Jerrold J. Katz, "Semantics and conceptual change," *Philosophical Review* 88 (1979): 362.

the augustinian *cogito*

We saw in chapter 3 that Augustine in his very early work *Against the Academicians* established that we can know how the perceptible world and things within it *seem* to us, even if we can never know how they actually are. I mentioned that Augustine in his later writings shows relatively little interest in this source of knowledge. Still, he retains an interest in showing that, contrary to the skeptics, there are many important things we can actually *know*. His most innovative and significant example of something he says that each of us can know is what we each express individually by saying, "I exist."

There is almost no hint in *Against the Academicians* of the idea that 'I know I exist' might count as an important knowledge claim, or even that 'I exist' might count as a genuine item of knowledge by Zeno's definition. But by the time we get to Augustine's last great work, the *City of God*, 'I exist' and 'I know that I exist' are paradigm knowledge claims. Here is the crucial passage:

> T1. In respect of those truths the quibbles of the Academicians [i.e., the skeptics of the New Academy] lose their force. If they say, "What if you are mistaken?" – well, if I am mistaken, I am. For one who does not exist can by no means be mistaken. Therefore, I am, if I am mistaken. Because, therefore, if I am mistaken I am [*si fallor sum*] how can I be mistaken [in thinking] that I am, since it is certain that I am if I am mistaken. And because, if I could be mistaken, I would have to be the one who is mistaken, therefore I am most certainly not mistaken in knowing that I am. (11.26)

I call the idea expressed in this passage "the Augustinian *cogito*" to bring out an important similarity between it and Descartes's much more famous reasoning, *cogito ergo sum* (I think, therefore I am). For purposes of comparison, here is one of the two most important Cartesian *cogito* passages. This one is from his *Second Meditation*:

> T2. . . . I have convinced myself that there is absolutely nothing in the world, no sky, no earth, no minds, no bodies. Does it follow that I too do not exist? No: if I convinced myself of something [the French version adds:

... or thought anything at all] then I certainly existed. But [suppose] there is a deceiver of supreme power and cunning, who is deliberately and constantly deceiving me. In that case I too undoubtedly am, if he deceives me [*sum, si me fallit*]; and let him deceive me as much as he can, he will never bring it about that I am nothing so long as I think that I am something. So after considering everything very thoroughly, I must finally conclude that this proposition, *I am, I exist*, is necessarily true whenever it is put forward by me or conceived in my mind. (CSM II, 16–17; AT VII, 25)

One central claim in the Augustinian passage, T1, is 'If I am mistaken, I am' (*si fallor, sum*). That claim almost exactly parallels the central claim in T2, the Cartesian passage, 'I am, if he deceives me' (*sum, si me fallit*). What is one to make of this remarkable similarity?

Commentators from Descartes's own time down to the present have concerned themselves with the question of what ideas Descartes borrowed from Augustine and, more generally, how much, and in what ways, Augustine influenced Descartes. Without doubt there was some significant influence. Philosophically much more interesting than the question of possible influence, however, is the question of what role Augustine assigns to the knowledge he thinks each of us has that we exist, and how that role compares with Descartes's use of the claim 'I exist.'

Descartes, in Part 4 of his *Discourse on Method*, presents his *cogito* reasoning this way:

T3. I noticed that while I was thus trying to think everything false, it was necessary that I, who was thinking this, was something. And observing that this truth 'I think, therefore I am' was so firm and sure that all the most extravagant suppositions of the skeptics were incapable of shaking it, I decided that I could accept it without scruple as the first principle of the philosophy I was seeking. (CSM I, 127; AT VI, 32)

As Descartes makes clear in T3, he uses 'I exist' as the first principle of the philosophy he is seeking. His procedure, in the *Meditations*, is roughly this. He finds 'I exist' invulnerable to doubt. Because of its invulnerability to doubt it becomes the foundation stone in his rational reconstruction of what it is that he knows. Next, he asks what this 'I' that cannot doubt that it exists is. It is, he answers, something that doubts, understands, affirms, denies, is willing, is unwilling, and also imagines and has sensory impressions, in short, it is a mind, a thinking thing (*res cogitans*).

Descartes next asks what is so special about his idea that he exists that makes it invulnerable to doubt. His answer is that this idea is *clear and distinct*. He then accepts clarity and distinctness as a criterion of truth ("whatever I perceive very clearly and distinctly is true"). With this criterion in hand he undertakes to prove the existence and nature of God and, in the last *Meditation*, the existence of the physical world of body. It is thus true that Descartes makes 'I exist' the first principle of his philosophy.

Can we find anything comparable to this rational reconstruction of knowledge on the indubitable foundation of 'I exist' in Augustine? There is, in fact, a dim foreshadowing of Descartes's project in Book 2 of Augustine's *On Free Choice of the Will*. I quoted a bit from it in chapter 1, where Augustine helps his interlocutor, Evodius, reconstruct what he knows about himself and the world. That project, which begins with Evodius's acceptance of the claim 'I exist,' culminates in an argument for the existence of God.

One has to admit, however, that Augustine's reconstruction project in Book 2 of *On Free Choice of the Will* is nowhere nearly as systematic, ambitious, or compelling as Descartes's project in his *Meditations*. Augustine's project does invite Evodius, and through him, each of us, his readers, to think about what we know on the basis of our own experience and reasoning, without appeal to outside authority. But one cannot say much more for it.

The other *cogito* passages in Augustine, however, most notably the passage from the *City of God*, T1, and an especially fascinating passage from *On the Trinity*, Book 15, are much more sophisticated defenses of Augustine's knowledge that he exists. But they do not lead to anything so ambitious as a proof of the existence of God. What purpose do they serve?

For one thing, these later passages hark back to the project of *Against the Academicians*: to show that global or universal skepticism can be defeated. Although Augustine does not bring up the topic of Zeno's definition in these later works, it seems likely that he himself is working with a similar conception of knowledge, no doubt one freed from the mental machinery of "kataleptic" or cognitive, that is, knowledge-producing, impressions. His notion of knowledge seems to be well captured in the following biconditional, which is a close relative of (Z), my attempt in chapter 3 to capture the core of Zeno's definition:

(K) A knows that p if, and only if, (i) it seems to A that p and
     (ii) A cannot be mistaken in thinking that p.

Consider now 'I exist.' It certainly seems to me that I exist, so condition (1) of (K) is satisfied. Moreover, in thinking that I exist I cannot be mistaken. So condition (2) of (K) is satisfied. Thus, by (K), I know that I exist.

(K) works a little more smoothly than (Z) with some of Augustine's other examples in *Against the Academicians*. Consider the arithmetical truth that $2 + 2 = 4$. By (K) I know that $2 + 2 = 4$ if (1) it seems to me that $2 + 2 = 4$ and (2) in thinking that $2 + 2 = 4$ I cannot be mistaken. The second claim seems more natural than what we would have to come up with for (Z), namely, 'it couldn't seem to me that $2 + 2 = 4$ unless $2 + 2$ did $= 4$.' In any case, let us work with (K) as a good approximation to Augustine's criterion for knowledge, at least in his later works.

I called attention in chapter 3 to a difference between the way a truth of logic or mathematics might be known, according to (Z), and the way a truth of sensory appearance might be known. 'This tastes bitter to me' is known to me by its seeming to taste bitter, plus the impossibility of its both seeming that this tastes bitter to me and its not being the case that this is bitter to me. By contrast, '$2 + 2 = 4$' is known to me, one could say, simply by its seeming to me that $2 + 2 = 4$, plus its being impossible that $2 + 2 \neq 4$. What guarantees the truth of what seems to me to be the case in that instance is the necessity of '$2 + 2 = 4$.'

In this respect, 'I exist' is a little more like 'This tastes bitter to me.' It is not necessarily true that I, GM, exist, even though, as Descartes tells us in T2, 'I exist' is necessarily true "whenever it is put forward by me or conceived in my mind."

Sense-datum philosophers of the twentieth century claimed that infallible perceptions of appearances (e.g., 'it looks red to me,' 'it tastes bitter to me') are the foundation of what we know about the perceptual world. Augustine, however, was not a sense-datum theorist. He had no special philosophical interest in the appearances of things. Thus it is not surprising that, when he came on the idea that one could defeat the threat of global skepticism with 'I exist,' he should have dropped 'It tastes bitter to me' and 'It looks red to me' as important specimen items of knowledge, impregnable to doubt. 'I exist' is surely a much more significant item.

There is, however, considerably more to say about the role of 'I exist' in the philosophy of Augustine.[1] Note how Augustine introduces his *cogito* reasoning in the *City of God*:

> T4. We too, as a matter of fact, recognize in ourselves an image of God, that is of this most high Trinity, even if the Image is not equal to Him in worth, but rather very far short of being so. The image is not co-eternal and, to sum the matter up briefly, it is not formed of the same substance of God. Yet it is nearer to him in the scale of nature than any other thing created by him, although it still requires to be reshaped and perfected in order to be nearest to him in its likeness to him also. For we exist, and we know that we exist, and we love to exist and to know that we exist.
>
> In these three things I have said, moreover, we are not confused by any mistake masquerading as truth. For we do not get in touch with these realities, as we do with external objects, by means of any bodily sense. We know colors, for instance, by seeing them, sounds by hearing them, odors

by smelling them, the taste of things by tasting them, and hard and soft objects by feeling them. We also have images that closely resemble these physical objects, but they are not material. They live in our minds, where we use them in thinking, preserve them in our memory, and are stimulated by them to desire the objects themselves. But it is without any deceptive play of my imagination, with its real or unreal visions, that I am quite certain that I am, that I know that I am, and that I love this being and this knowing. (*City of God* 11.26)

T4 is an incredibly audacious passage. It compares each of us human beings to the Divine Trinity. In fact it encapsulates the central idea of Books 8 through 15 of Augustine's great treatise *On the Trinity*. In that work Augustine tries to help us understand how God can be both three and one by coming up with various "trinities" of the human mind, such as memory, understanding, and will, and getting us to realize that these trinities are also both three and one. His idea is that the mind is memory, understanding, and will in a way somewhat analogous to the way God is Father, Son, and Holy Spirit. Crudely put, memory is not just part of mind, say, a compartment of mind or a faculty of mind; nor is understanding or will just a compartment or faculty of mind. Memory is the mind, even if it is not all there is to mind. Memory is the mind recollecting things. Understanding is the mind comprehending things. And will is the mind in choosing things and putting things into action.

In T4 Augustine thinks he finds another sort of analogy to illuminate the three-in-oneness of God. This time his trinity is the three truths 'I am,' 'I know that I am,' and 'I love to be and to know that I am.' Each is distinct from the other two, but none is separate from the other two.

All this is a rather arcane way of inviting us to reflect on the "inner sphere" of our being, to which not just the initial triple of truths 'I am,' 'I know that I am,' and 'I love to be and to know that I am' apply, but a whole flock of additional truths as well. This "inner" realm is, he thinks, immediately and directly known to each of us. It is something to which we each, individually, have what later philosophers call "privileged access." And it is quite distinct from the "external" world revealed only imperfectly to us through our senses. Augustine thinks that 'I exist' is a central truth of this inner knowledge. Other truths rest, somehow, on this fundamental truth.

Here now is what comes right after T1:

T5. It follows also that in saying that I know that I know, I am not mistaken. For just as I know that I am, so it holds too that I know that I know. And when I love these two things, I add this same love as a third particular of no smaller value to these things that I know. Nor is my statement that I love a mistake, since I am not mistaken in the things that I love. Even if they were illusions, it would still be true that I love illusions. (*City of God* 11.26)

It would take considerable discussion to sort out the basis on which Augustine thinks he can multiply the truths he supposes he can know about his inner self. For one thing, he *seems* to suppose he can help himself to what is called today the "KK Principle," namely, 'If A knows that p, then A knows that s/he knows that p.'

Jaakko Hintikka, in his pioneering work on epistemic logic *Knowledge and Belief* (Ithaca: Cornell University Press, 1962), claims that '*a* knows that *a* knows that *p*' is "virtually equivalent" to '*a* knows that *p*.' His reasoning is that it would, after all, be odd to say, "I know that this is Herter Hall, but I don't know that I know it."

I agree so far. It certainly would be odd to say, "I know that this is Herter Hall, but I don't know that I know it." But, as G. E. Moore pointed out long ago, it would also be odd to say, "This is Herter Hall, but I don't believe this is Herter Hall." Yet we do not want to say that 'I believe this is Herter Hall' is virtually equivalent to 'This is Herter Hall.' We do not even want to say that 'This is Herter Hall' entails 'I believe that this is Herter Hall.' At most we want to say that someone's *saying*, "This is Herter Hall," in normal circumstances pragmatically implies, or conversationally implies, that the speaker believes that this is Herter Hall.

We should, I think, be wary of assuming that 'I know that I exist' is "virtually equivalent" to 'I know that I know that I exist.' In normal circumstances it would be very odd to say the first thing without agreeing to the second. But let's imagine an abnormal circumstance. Suppose I am unsure about what is required for some belief of mine to count as knowledge. I might say, "Well, whatever is required for knowledge, I am entirely sure of this: I know that I exist. But until I get clear about the proper analysis of knowledge, I cannot honestly say, 'I know that I know that I exist.'"

As a matter of fact, defending Augustine's "ascent" from 'I know that I exist' to 'I know that I know that I exist' on the ground that these two claims are virtually equivalent should not be welcome to Augustine anyway. After all, his project is to multiply the truths one can be said to know concerning the "inner sphere" of one's mind without fear of skeptical challenge. If the higher level knowledge claims are virtually equivalent to the basic knowledge claim, then the multiplication will be only an illusory enlargement of one's "inner knowledge," or perhaps a "virtual enlargement" of it.

Augustine's idea must be, not that the iterated knowledge claim ('I know that I know . . .') is equivalent, even virtually equivalent, to the uniterated claim, but rather that knowing that one knows that one exists is something that can seem to one to be the case in such a way that one cannot be mistaken. But just why he thinks this is not clear to me.

Let us turn now to the *cogito* passage in *On the Trinity*. It resembles T1 and T5, but with one striking and obvious difference. In it Augustine uses "I am alive' (or 'I live') in place of 'I am' (or 'I exist'). For 'I am alive' to play this central role as an item of "inner knowledge" we must understand 'life' and 'alive' and their cognates, not in any specifically biological sense, but rather in the way we naturally understand 'life' in the question 'Is there life after death?' As that question is normally understood, an affirmative answer might be supported by evidence of some post-mortem form of conscious existence that failed to have any biological basis.

Here is the key passage from *On the Trinity*:

> T6. It is an inner knowledge by which we know that we live, where not even the Academician can say: "Perhaps you are sleeping, and you do not know, and you see in dreams." For who does not know that things seen by those who are asleep are very similar to things seen by those who are awake. But he who is certain about the knowledge of his own life does not say in it: "I know that I am awake," but "I know that I live"; whether he, therefore, sleeps or whether he is awake, he lives. He cannot be deceived in his knowledge of this even by dreams, because to sleep and to see in dreams is characteristic of one who lives. . . . Let a thousand kinds of optical illusions be placed before one who says: "I know that I live"; he will fear none of them, since even he who is deceived, lives. (15.12.21)

This passage, like T1, is followed immediately by a passage in which Augustine seeks to multiply the items of inner knowledge that are, he supposes, similarly immune to the attacks of the skeptics:

> T7. If such things alone belong to human knowledge, then they are very few; unless it be that they are so multiplied that they are not only a few, but are even found to reach an infinite number. For he who says: "I know that I live," says that he knows one thing; if he were then to say: "I know that I know that I live," there are already two things, but that he knows these two, is to know a third thing; and so he can add a fourth and a fifth, and innumerable more, as long as he is able to do so. But because he cannot comprehend an innumerable number by adding one thing to another, or to express a thing innumerable times, he comprehends this very fact and says with absolute certainty that this is both true and so innumerable that he cannot truly comprehend and express its infinite number. (15.12.21)

Augustine goes on after T7 to make similar claims about 'I will (or want) to be happy.' That claim, he says, is something one cannot be deceived about.[2] And he adds that, just as I know I want to be happy, so I know that I know I want to be happy, and so on.

Exactly how Augustine thinks the iteration of knowledge claims ('I know that I know that I know,' etc.) can be justified in the face of the most ardent skepticism is unclear to me. At least three difficulties stand in the way of using the KK Principle to justify these iterations.

The first difficulty I have already mentioned. If the KK Principle is itself justified by supposing that 'I know that I know that p' is virtually equivalent to 'I know that p,' then the multiplication of knowledge claims may be only an illusion, each iteration being virtually equivalent to its predecessor.

A second difficulty afflicts third-person instantiations of the KK Principle. Jane may know that p, but not know that Jane knows that p because she does not know that she is Jane. This difficulty seems not to apply to first-person applications of the KK Principle, since I cannot fail to know that I am I (or more colloquially: that I am me).

The third difficulty, which I have also already alluded to, may be the most serious of the three. Suppose I know that I exist all right, but I have become troubled by the inability of philosophers to agree on what it is to know something. It seems I cannot know that I know that I exist unless I know what it is to know something. If I know anything, and surely I do know something, I know that I exist. But to *know that I know* I exist I must also, it may well seem, know what are the necessary and sufficient conditions for knowing something. And this I do not know.

Augustine seems not to share any of my qualms. He seems quite confident that he is justified in iterating these "inner knowledge" claims without making himself vulnerable to skeptical attack. It seems to be important for him to do this so that he can give a central place to inner knowledge, alongside knowledge from the senses and from testimony. Thus the long discussion of 'I know that I am alive' and 'I know that I want to be happy,' and their innumerable iterations is followed in *On the Trinity* by a passage in which he compares these claims to inner knowledge to other, more conventional knowledge claims:

> T8. Far be it from us to doubt the truth of those things we have perceived through the senses of the body. For through them we have learned of the heavens and the earth, and those things in them which are known to us insofar as He, who had created us and them, wanted them to become known to us.
>
> Far be it also from us to deny what we have learned from the testimony of others; otherwise, we would not know that there is an ocean; we would not know that there are lands and cities which the most celebrated fame commends; we would not know of the men and their works which we learned in the reading of history; we would not know the news that is daily brought to us from everywhere, and is confirmed by evidence that is consistent and convincing; finally, we would not know in what places and from what persons we are born; because we have believed all these things on the testimony of others. But it is most absurd to deny this, and we must confess that, not only the senses of our own bodies, but also those of other persons have added very much to our knowledge. (15.12.21)

Considered by itself, T8 is a very ordinary list of things we commonly take ourselves to know. But in the context of a discussion of reasoning remarkably similar to Descartes's *cogito*, it is most remarkable. What T8 makes clear, beyond the shadow of a doubt, is that Augustine has here no ambition whatsoever to provide a rational reconstruction of all he knows on the indubitable foundation of 'I exist' (or 'I know that I exist') or 'I am alive' (or 'I know that I am alive'). Instead he uses 'I know that I am alive' and the iteration of knowledge claims he thinks follow from it, as well as 'I know that I want to be happy' and the iteration of knowledge claims he thinks follow from it to call attention to an inner realm of knowledge each of us has open to us. It is a realm, he thinks, that is invulnerable to Academic skepticism. But in no way does he suppose that this realm of inner knowledge is the foundation for all that we know. What we know from our senses of the heavens and the earth and what we know from testimony of others about human history and our own personal history is neither to be denigrated nor to be given a philosophical foundation by our inner knowledge.

Looking back to Augustine's *On Free Choice of the Will*, we can perhaps see in it some foreshadowing of Descartes's audacious attempt to reconstruct all he knows on the invulnerable foundation of 'I think, therefore I exist.' But if Augustine ever had a project anywhere nearly as ambitious as Descartes's, he abandoned it later in life.

further reading

Gareth B. Matthews, *Thought's Ego in Augustine and Descartes*. Ithaca: Cornell University Press, 1992. This work offers a more extensive comparison of the aims and accomplishments of Augustine and Descartes.

notes

1 I owe the appreciation of this point to Charles Brittain.
2 We shall discuss in chapter 15 whether one can be mistaken or deceived about the desire for happiness.

mind–body dualism

In Book 10 of Augustine's great treatise *On the Trinity* we can find at least two different arguments for mind–body dualism. Augustine may have thought of himself as offering a single line of reasoning for the immateriality of the mind. But these two arguments seem quite distinct. Moreover, each argument is quite different from anything one can find on the real distinction between mind and body in Descartes. And both are different from the arguments for the incorporeality of the soul in Plato as well.

Here is the first argument:

T1. All these [philosophers] fail to notice that the mind [*mens*] knows itself, even when it seeks itself, . . . But in no way is something correctly said to be known when its substance [or essence, *substantia*] is unknown. Therefore, as long as the mind knows itself, it knows its substance [or essence]. But it is certain about itself, as the things said above have proved. But it is by no means certain whether it is air, or fire, or a body, or anything bodily. It is not, therefore, any of these. (10.10.16)

What, exactly, does Augustine mean when he writes in this passage that the mind "is certain of itself [*certa de se*], as the things said above have proved"? Perhaps he is referring to a passage in chapter 9 of the same work, section 12, which begins this way:

T2. But when it is said to the mind: "Know thyself!" it knows itself at the very instant in which it understands the word 'thyself'; and it knows itself for no other reason than that it is present to itself. But if it does not understand what is said, it certainly does not obey this command. Accordingly it is commanded to do what it does when it understands the command itself. (10.9.12)

Augustine goes on:

T3. Let [the mind] not add anything to that which it itself knows when it hears that it should know itself. For it certainly knows itself to be spoken to, itself, that is, which exists and lives and understands. But a corpse exists and a beast lives; however, neither a corpse nor a beast understands. Therefore [the mind] knows itself to exist and live in the way that understanding [*intellegentia*] exists and lives. (10.10.13)

What, one might well wonder, is "the way in which understanding exists and lives"? What Augustine seems to have in mind is the way the characteristic activity of the mind goes on. Thus the way in which intelligence exists and lives seems to be the way in which conscious thinking exists and lives.

A materialist, Augustine goes on, must think it is matter of some sort that does the understanding. But that is just an opinion, something that philosophers disagree about. Yet even if some materialist philosopher's mind thinks it is itself air, or fire, or anything bodily, that would be, at most, something it believes about itself, nothing that it knows to be true of itself. "Let us, therefore, separate off," he writes, "that which it [merely] thinks itself to be and consider only that which it knows [itself to be]." Thus:

T4. Let this remain to it, which not even they have doubted who regarded the mind as this or that kind of body. For not every mind regards itself as air, but, as I mentioned above, some regard it as fire, others as a brain, and others as this or that kind of body. All know, however, that they understand and exist and live . . . (10.10.13)

Augustine next makes this important methodological move:

T5. But since we treat of the nature of the mind, let us remove from our consideration all knowledge which is received from without, through the senses of the body, and attend more carefully to the position which we have laid down, that all minds know and are certain concerning themselves. (10.10.14)

Augustine continues:

T6. For people have certainly doubted whether the power of living, remembering, understanding, willing, thinking, knowing, judging, were of air, or of fire, or of the brain, or of the blood, or of atoms, or besides the usual four elements, of a fifth kind of body – I know not what – or whether the combining or tempering together of this our flesh itself has the power to accomplish these things. And one has attempted to establish this, and another to establish that. Yet whoever doubts that he himself lives, and remembers, and understands, and wills, and thinks, and knows, and judges? (10.10.14)

Augustine's list of indubitable mental functions becomes his characterization of what a mind is. Thus:

M. A mind is something that lives, remembers, understands, wills, thinks, knows, and judges.

Augustine seeks to establish this list by showing that the mind's very attempt to doubt that it performs any one of these functions is, in a certain way, self-defeating.

All this brings us back to our first passage, T1. We have learned, I think, what Augustine means when he says that the mind "knows itself" and "is certain about itself, as the things said above have proved." The mind knows that it exists, lives, and understands. The mind also knows that it has the nature given in M. Now here is the argument to prove that the mind is not a body, or anything bodily:

Argument A

(1) If x knows and is certain of y, then x knows the substance [or essence] of y.

Thus: (2) If the mind knows and is certain of y, then it knows the substance [or essence] of y.

(3) If x knows the substance [or essence] of y, then for any matter or kind of matter, z, if y is z, then x is certain that y is z.

Thus: (4) If the mind knows its own substance [or essence], then if it is air, or fire, or any body, or anything bodily, the mind is certain that it is air, or fire, or some body, or something bodily.

But: (5) The mind is not certain that it is air, or fire, or any body, or anything bodily.

So: (6) The mind is none of these.

We may be somewhat unsure about how to translate *substantia* in T1, since Augustine tells us in Book 5[1] of this very same work that his Latin makes no distinction between *substantia* (substance), and *essentia* (essence). Let us try to keep both options open.

The weakest point in Argument A seems to be premise (1). If we translate *substantia* as substance, the meaning might be that one cannot know something without being able to at least identify its substance. Thus the application to mind, line (2) in the argument, might require only that, in knowing itself, the mind would need to know that it is a mind. But that reading would not seem to underwrite line (4). Why should we think that any mind that knows that it is a mind will thereby know what material, if any, it is made of?

Perhaps Augustine had anticipated this objection when, in the passage immediately preceding T1, he had conceded that the materialist will consider the activities of the mind as a configuration of qualities – properties, we might say today – of a material substance. But he does nothing there to make plausible the claim that, by knowing and being certain of itself, the mind, if it were a configuration of properties of some substance, would have to know and be certain what substance it is a configuration of properties *of*.

Since understanding *substantia* to be substance has not yielded a persuasive argument, perhaps we should use the other option and let 'essence' be our translation of *substantia*. It would indeed seem more plausible to claim that any mind that knows its essence will also be certain whether it is air, or fire, or any body. However, though more plausible, it may still not be plausible enough. Perhaps, as some philosophers have thought, the mind is a functional entity that can be realized in any one of several different materials. On this view the mind can certainly be realized in a brain, but perhaps it can also be realized in computer hardware, or in some other material. If this is right, then a mind might know its own essence without knowing what matter it is realized in.

On this "essence" interpretation of *substantia*, moreover, line (1) also seems implausible. Why should we suppose that anyone who knows x, will know the essence of x? To choose Aristotle's famous example in *Posterior Analytics* B8, it seems one could know thunder is a noise in the clouds without knowing the essence of thunder. Indeed, as Aristotle suggests in that passage, one might need to use a "nominal definition," such as 'noise in the clouds,' to identify the thing one is trying to determine the essence of.

Thus, whichever way we understand *substantia* in line (1) and following, that premise of Argument A seems questionable. My conclusion, then, is that Argument A is unpersuasive.

Augustine also has a second argument for mind–body dualism. The passage in which he offers this argument follows directly on the passage quoted above. It goes this way:

> T7. For just as the [mind] thinks of [*cogitat*] fire, so it thinks of air, or any other bodily thing. Nor could it in any way happen that it would think of that which it itself is in the same way as it thinks of that which itself is not. For it thinks of these things – whether fire, or air, or this or that body, or that part or combination or harmony of the body – by means of an imaginary phantasy [*per phantasiam imaginariam*]; nor is it said [by philosophers] to be all of these things, but some one of them. But if [the mind] were any one of them, it would think of this one in a different manner from [the way it thinks of] the rest. That is to say, it would not think of it by means of an image figment [*per imaginale figmentum*], as absent things through which it has been touched by the sense of the body, but it would think about it by a kind of inward presence, not simulated [*simulata*] but real (for there is not anything more present to it than it itself), just as it thinks itself to live, and to remember, and to understand, and to will. And if it adds nothing from thoughts of these [other things] to itself, so as to regard itself

as some such thing, then whatever remains to it of itself, this alone it itself is. (10.10.16)

The argument Augustine presents here turns on his understanding of how we bring things to mind. Although he does not mention here the possibility of thinking about something we perceive through the senses, he certainly does suppose we can do that. Indeed, in the next book, Book 11 of *On the Trinity*, Augustine talks about how the "attention of the mind" can fix the sense on the thing we see and hold the sense and the thing we see together (11.2.2). In this way I can look at a tree, or a mountain, or the sea, and think about what I am seeing as I am seeing it. I can also listen to music and think about the music just as I am hearing it.

Suppose that I come to think about what I saw or heard this morning when the tree is no longer visible to me and the music is no longer audible. In that case, Augustine supposes, I can think of the tree or the music by entertaining the memory images I have available to me.

Suppose now that someone tells me something about a tree I have never myself seen, or about a piece of music I have never myself heard. In that case, Augustine thinks, I can make up a mental image of what is being described to me and perhaps succeed that way in thinking of what I have not seen or heard. Thus consider this passage:

T8. The only reason I could understand what the narrator was saying was because I remembered generically the individual things that he described. For example, he who describes to me a mountain that is stripped of its forest and clothed with olive trees is speaking to one who remembers the forms of the mountains, the forests, and the olive trees; had I forgotten them, I should not at all know what he was saying . . . everyone who conceives corporeal things, whether he himself forms an image of them or whether he hears or reads what someone relates about the past or foretells about the future, returns to his memory and finds there the mode and the measure of all the forms that he beholds in his thoughts. (11.8.14)

To be sure, Augustine thinks there are limits to what one can imagine successfully. One must have in the storehouse of one's memory the appropriate components to form a successful image of whatever it is one is to imagine.[2] But, so long as one can recall having had sense experience of the right sorts, one's mind can make up images of things one has never seen and music one has never heard.

For the project of bringing fire to mind I would need, Augustine will suppose, either a memory image of seeing flames, or a memory image of having seen a picture of flames. Thinking of air will also require a mental image, this time, perhaps, the image of feeling air on one's skin, or perhaps the sound of it leaving a balloon. In any case, it is his view that we need a mental representation to succeed in thinking of anything corporeal.

Now when Augustine says in T7 that the mind thinks of itself without the aid of an imaginary phantasy, his claim is that the mind needs no image whatsoever to think of itself. That result, he thinks, is a consequence of the fact that nothing is so present to the mind as the mind itself. The mind is immediately, in particular, without the mediation of any image, maximally present to itself.

There has been much debate in recent philosophy and psychology about whether we really need mental images to think of physical things in their absence. Through the influence of Wittgenstein and others, many philosophers have concluded that having images is inessential to having thoughts, even about physical things. After all, some subjects report sincerely that they can think quite successfully of mountains and houses and people without having any images at all. Even if others maintain they cannot achieve such a feat, we obviously do not need to know whether our conversation partner has a mental image of Grandma to assure ourselves that we can have the same person in mind when, as we think, we are both talking and thinking about Grandma.

The current view that having images is inessential to thinking of physical entities or physical stuffs when one is not actually perceiving them with the senses rejects an assumption that goes back to ancient philosophy. Does rejecting that assumption undercut Augustine's argument for the immateriality of the mind? I do not think so. The role of mental images in Augustine's account of how we can think about a physical thing in its absence is the role of mental representations. A mental image, however, is only one kind of mental representation, and not the only kind. A description is another kind of representation. The more general point would seem to be that, according to Augustine, we cannot have a physical thing in mind without having in mind some sort of mental representation of whatever it is we are thinking about. This would then be his thesis:

N. The mind cannot think of a physical object or of any physical material except by having a mental representation of that object or stuff.

Here again is the crucial part of passage T7:

> T7*. But if [the mind] were any one of them [that is, any one of the many physical things some philosopher or other has said that the mind is, such as fire, air, or anything of the sort] it would think of this in a manner different from [the way it thinks of] the rest. That is to say, it would not think of it by means of an image figment, . . . but it would think of it by a kind of inward presence, not simulated but real (for there is not anything more present to it than it itself), just as it thinks itself to live, and to remember, and to understand, and to will.

What does Augustine actually mean by saying that "nothing is more present to the mind than it is present to itself"? At a minimum, he seems to mean that the mind is directly aware of itself, without any intermediary, that is, without having to represent itself to itself. Thus it need not think of itself, he says, "by means of an image figment" or *simulacrum*. It can be directly, immediately, aware of itself, as it is when it thinks of itself that it lives, remembers, understands, and wills.

The way the mind is aware of itself, Augustine tells us, is by its "real presence" to itself. Nothing is more present to it, he tells us, than it is present to itself. Since the mind is, according to Augustine, present to itself to the maximum degree, I shall say that, according to him, the mind is "fully present" to itself.

What exactly is the argument in T7? To get a handle on what Augustine may be up to in this passage we might begin by reminding ourselves that the objects we think about may be either singular or general. Thus I can think about my very own horse or my very own barn, or I can think about a horse in general, or a barn in general, without thinking about any particular horse or barn.

The example Augustine begins with in Book 8 of *On the Trinity* is the apostle Paul. Augustine says we love Paul. But, he asks, is it the human form we believe him to have had that we love? No, he answers; it is rather his rational soul, or mind [*animus*]. There then follows a explanation of how it is we can, each of us, know that there are individual rational souls in addition to our own. The explanation Augustine offers is, so far as I know, the first statement of what has come to be called "the argument from analogy for other minds" (8.6.9).

In the next book, Book 9 of the *On the Trinity*, Augustine focuses his attention specifically on *mens*, mind, rather than on *anima*, soul, or even on *animus*, rational soul. I have translated *mens* as "the mind," but, of course, in Augustine's Latin there are no articles, either definite or indefinite. It is quite clear, however, that when Augustine talks about *mens*, "the mind," he means for what he says to apply to particular minds, singulars, for example, St. Paul's mind, your mind, and mine.

Thus when Augustine talks about the mind thinking of itself, he means for what he says to be true of how my mind and your mind think of themselves. The question of how a mind can know singulars is, of course, a familiar problem in philosophy, especially, perhaps, of the philosophy of the High Middle Ages. I cannot here outline what I take to be Augustine's full account of our knowledge of singulars. I'll just say that, in the case of my knowledge of animate or inanimate physical objects, such as my one and only horse and my one and only barn, the account will make a prominent place for the phantasms or mental images I have, and of their causal history.

How does my mind manage to think of itself in particular, rather than, say, St. Paul's mind, or mind in general? "Each individual human being, attentive to what is going on within him," Augustine writes at 9.6.9, "speaks in one way when he states his own mind, but marks off the human mind [in general] in a different way by the knowledge of [its] species or genus."

So how does my individual or singular mind manage to think of itself in particular? Augustine's answer is clearly that the mind thinks of itself simply by being fully present to itself, that is, fully aware of itself. So now we have this argument for mind–body dualism:

Argument B

(1) Each individual mind can think of itself simply by being fully present to itself, that is, by being fully aware of itself.
Therefore,
(2) Each individual mind can be fully present to itself, that is, fully aware of itself.
(3) If each individual mind were a particular mass of air or volume of fire or other material stuff, that particular mass or volume of stuff could be fully present to itself, that is, fully aware of itself.
(4) No particular mass of air or volume of material stuff can be fully present to itself, that is, fully aware of itself.
Therefore,
(5) No individual mind is a particular mass of air or volume of material stuff.

Line (3) seems quite defensible, given line (2). Line (2) tells us about individual minds that each one can be fully present to itself. Line (3) then adds that if each individual mind were a particular mass of material, what is true of each mind would also be true of that mass of material. There seems to be no problem here of substituting in intentional or opaque contexts. The conditional identity claim seems to be a claim of extensional identity. So there should be no logical problem with the inference.

What about line (4)? If my mind were my brain, my brain would be aware of whatever my mind is aware of. So would my brain be fully aware of, or present to, itself? Well, it would not be aware of its molecular structure, for example. It need not even be aware that it is a brain. So (4) seems quite acceptable.

I conclude that this is a pretty good argument. I also think that the reasoning is based on assumptions Augustine makes in *On the Trinity* 10. Nevertheless, I am not confident that this reasoning is to be found in Augustine. In particular, my reconstruction does not seem to fit passage T7 very well. After all, the talk in T7 is about how, if the mind were one of these kinds of material that materialist philosophers have said it is, it would think about that kind of material in a different way from the rest. Argument B does not make use of that idea. Rather, according to Argument B, if the mind were one of these kinds of material, *that material would think of itself in a different way*. And that is not what Augustine says in T7. So we should try again.

Here is an attempt to stay closer to the text of T7:

Argument C

(1) If the mind were made of some kind of physical stuff, then the mind, simply by being fully present to itself, would think of the physical stuff it is made of.
(2) The mind, simply by being fully present to itself, does not think of any physical stuff.
Therefore,
(3) The mind is not made of any kind of physical stuff.

This is the best way I can think of to make sense of Augustine's suggestion that if the mind were of any such material as the various materialist philosophers have suggested that it is, it would think of this material "in a different way from the rest" [*aliter id quam cetera cogitaret*]. His idea seems to be that, in thinking of itself, not by a mental picture or representation, but simply by being maximally present to itself, the stuff, if any, it were made of would have to be present to itself as well. Since no such stuff is present to the mind simply by the mind's being present to itself, it is not made of any material stuff.

Perhaps the greatest challenge to the idea of full mental self-presence, and hence to the reasoning I have tried to capture in Argument C, comes, not from materialist theories of the mind, but from the idea of the *unconscious* mind. We post-Freudians, or anyway most of us, are convinced that many of our beliefs and desires are *not* fully present to our minds. After all, we may have to go through a tortuous process to come to recognize that we harbor malevolent thoughts and desires toward people we want to think of ourselves as loving or respecting.

Augustine, I think, did not conceive that there might be unconscious beliefs or desires. To him it seems obvious that the mind is fully available to its own self-reflections. Does acceptance of the idea of a partially unconscious mind simply derail Argument C?

I do not think so. We can point out that even unconscious beliefs and desires have to be, according to Freudian theory, somehow directly available to the thinking subject. I may at first resist the thought that I want to kill my father and marry my mother. But if it is really true that I have such desires, I must be able to avow those desires as my own rather than accept them, as a third party might, as the best explanation of my otherwise puzzling behavior. It may take me many years of analysis to come to the point of avowing those dark desires. But to say that they are truly mine is to say that, under ideal conditions of self-understanding, I would, if I were honest, acknowledge that I have them.

The materialist philosopher who tells me that my mind is made of air or fire or protoplasm may be able to get me to accept reasoning that leads to a materialist conclusion about what my mind is made of. But the materialist philosopher will not be able to get me to recognize, simply by the mind's full presence to itself, that my mind is made of some special kind of material. And so the Freudian challenge to Augustine's idea of the mind's full presence to itself can be plausibly rejected.

I am ready to plump for Argument C as the most plausible reading of T7 I can come up with and as Augustine's most persuasive argument for mind–body dualism. But here I must enter a warning. Even if Argument C were an entirely satisfactory argument for the immateriality of the mind, it, by itself, gives us no reason for concluding that the mind can exist separately and independently from any body. In this respect, among others, Augustine's reasoning is quite different from Descartes's. For all we know – at least for all we know from this argument – each mind needs to be seated in a body, perhaps in a brain, or in some brain-like structure. Given Augustine's own endorsement of the Christian doctrine of the resurrection of the body, the idea that a mind might need to be seated in a body to live and function in its own proper way need be no threat to belief in the afterlife. In any case, neither Argument C nor Argument B offers us a reason to suppose that the mind can exist and function all on its own. But, perhaps, that is as it should be. That is, perhaps Augustine would not want it otherwise.

further reading

John M. Rist, *Augustine: Ancient Thought Baptized*. Cambridge University Press, 1994, ch. 4 ("Soul, body and personal identity"). This chapter includes a broad survey of what Augustine has to say about minds or souls and bodies.

notes

1 At *On the Trinity* 5.9.10.
2 See, e.g., *On the Trinity* 11.10.17.

the problem of
other minds

A ugustine's great treatise, *On the Trinity*, is devoted, not to proving
that God is three-in-one, something Augustine does not think
he can do anyway, but rather to making sense of the idea. Much
of the first seven books of the work is aimed at establishing that the
doctrine is well founded in scripture. Most of the last eight books is
devoted to identifying and discussing mental or psychological trinities,
such as remembering, understanding, and willing, as analogies to the
Divine Trinity. Thus, as Augustine argues, (i) the mind as remembering
something, (ii) the mind as understanding something, and (iii) the mind
as willing something are each distinct, but they are one substance,
namely, the mind.

Early on in Book 9 we find this arresting passage:

T1. The mind cannot love its own self without knowing itself. For how
could it love that which it does not know? If someone says it is from either
a knowledge of the genus or of the species that the mind believes itself to
be such as it has experienced other minds to be, he speaks most foolishly.
For on what basis does the mind know another mind, if it does not know
itself? For it is not as the bodily eye sees other eyes and does not see itself,
that the mind knows other minds and does not know itself. (9.3.3)

It may seem strange to call T1 arresting. Does it not just raise the
familiar philosophical problem of other minds? I can observe a number
of swans on a pond, and, noting what features they have in common,
come up with the distinguishing characteristics of a swan. Can I, or can
my mind, observe a number of other minds and, after noting what characteristics they have in common, come up with the distinguishing characteristics of a mind? Of course not. To say that would be most foolish. I
cannot, it seems, even observe a single other mind, let alone a group of
them, to determine what qualities they have in common. The only mind
that my mind can observe is, it seems, itself. I cannot even observe, at

least not "directly," that anybody else *has* a mind! But does that problem not belong to Philosophy 101?

The problem of other minds is certainly a staple of modern philosophy. Yet it does not come up in the writings of Plato or Aristotle, or in the works of any of the other big names of ancient philosophy. T1 from Book 9 of Augustine's *On the Trinity* plus a companion passage in Book 8 of the same work may be the first places in Western philosophy in which the problem of other minds is broached.

The passage in Book 8 is even more explicit than T1, except that in the earlier passage Augustine uses the word *animus* (rational soul), instead of the word *mens* (mind), to state and try to solve the problem of other minds. I shall translate *animus* in Book 8 as "mind," but I shall mark the occurrences by giving the Latin term. I shall make a comment on the terminological shift in a moment.

Here is the first part of the relevant passage from Book 8:

> T2. And as regards the mind [*animus*], we not unfittingly say that we, therefore, know what a mind [*animus*] is because we also have a mind [*animus*]. We have never seen it with our eyes, nor formed a generic or specific idea of it from any similarity with other minds that we have seen, but rather, as I said, because we, too, have a mind [*animus*]. For what is so intimately known, and what so knows itself to be itself, as that through which all other things are likewise known, that is, the mind [*animus*] itself? (8.6.9)

Why does Augustine confuse us by using *animus* here, rather than *mens*, even though he shifts to *mens* in the next and following books?

I speculate that he begins with *animus* because he wants us to begin thinking of the mind, not as an entity primarily engaged in lofty speculations, but as the animator of a human body. As he is going to argue, I come to recognize minds in others by seeing an analogy between the way my own body moves in response to my own beliefs and desires, and the way other human bodies move. As he is going to point out, there is also an analogy between the bodily movements of nonrational animals – dogs, cats, cattle, sheep – and the movements of my body. But those actions are not the result of rational free choice. Nonhuman animals are animated by an *anima*, but not by an *animus*, a rational soul. Still, the analogy holds, even if only in an attenuated fashion.

He will move on to talk about *mens* when he focuses on self-consciousness. But, for now, he is thinking of the mind as a rational animator of a human body, an *animus*.

This is what immediately follows T2:

> T3. For we also recognize, from a likeness to us, the motions of bodies by which we perceive that others besides us live. Just as we move [our] body in living, so, we notice, those bodies are moved. For when a living body is

moved there is no way open to our eyes to see the mind [*animus*], a thing which cannot be seen by the eyes. But we perceive something present in that mass such as is present in us to move our mass in a similar way; it is life and soul [*anima*]. Nor is such perception something peculiar to, as it were, human prudence and reason. For indeed beasts perceive as living, not only themselves, but also each other and one another, and us as well. Nor do they see our souls [*animas*], except from the motions of the body, and they do that immediately and very simply by a sort of natural agreement. Therefore we know the mind of anyone at all from our own; and from our own case we believe in that which we do not know [*ex nostro credimus, quem non novimus*]. For not only do we perceive a mind, but we even know what one is, by considering our own; for we have a mind. (8.6.9)

So far as I know, these passages together, T1, T2, and T3, are not only the first statement of the problem of other minds in Western philosophy; they are also the first attempt to solve that problem. The solution is what in recent philosophy has come to be called the "Argument from Analogy for Other Minds."

It is good to be clear from the beginning that the problem of other minds is about how each of us can come to know that there is *another* mind besides our own. Thus it assumes an egocentric, or first-personal, starting point. To assume that there is only me, or my mind and its contents, is to be a *solipsist* (*solus*, only; *ipse*, myself). As a philosophical view, solipsism is pure madness. The philosophical importance of solipsism lies not in the attractiveness of the arguments proponents have marshaled to support it (no attractive arguments have ever been offered), but rather in the challenge to find arguments to reject it. That challenge is difficult to meet.

In any case, Augustine is not interested in discussing solipsism. He supposes, without offering any arguments to support the supposition, that there exists a world quite independently of him. What he thinks he needs to present is an argument for the conclusion that that world includes, not just his own mind, but other minds as well.

So the Argument from Analogy for Other Minds is not about refuting solipsism; it is about providing some rational basis for thinking, as we all do, that the world we assume exists quite independently of us includes, not just tables and chairs, mountains and forests, dogs and cows, but also minds in addition to one's own.

There is another philosophical problem about minds that can be, but should not be, confused with the problem of other minds. It is a problem about what *classes* or *kinds* of entities have, or might have, other minds. Is it just human beings? Or do other higher primates, say, chimps and gorillas, have minds? And what about monkeys? Or dogs? Or lizards? Or amoebas? And what about computers? The super computer, Deep Blue, beat Gary Kasparov at chess. Does Deep Blue have a mind? If Deep Blue does not, might some super-super computer, or robot, yet to be built have a mind? Philosophers have discussed this problem primarily as either the problem of *animal minds*, or as the problem of *minds and machines*.

It is interesting that Descartes, who never recognized the problem of other minds (more on that in a moment), did recognize the problem of animal minds and also the problem of minds and machines. Thus he did not see the need to recognize that there is a philosophical problem about how he could know there was another mind in addition to his own. But he did see the need to recognize and try to deal with the issue of whether any nonhuman animals have minds, and whether certain machines might have minds.

In T3 Augustine attributes to nonhuman animals a sort of instinctual recognition of other minds and souls that gives them what we might call "the functional equivalent" of the Argument from Analogy. It is not that, as he thinks, they reason their way to the conclusion that there are other minds; it is rather that, as he supposes, they recognize by a sort of "natural agreement" what we human beings – or at least the more philosophical among us – can capture rationally in the form of an argument for the conclusion that there are other minds.

This talk about nonhuman animals deploying the functional equivalent of the Argument from Analogy points up a further aspect of Augustine's thought that needs emphasis. Unlike Descartes, Augustine does not consider nonhuman animals to be mere automata. He attributes consciousness to them, but supposes they lack freedom of the will. They are thus not genuinely moral beings, according to Augustine, although their behavior often mimics genuinely moral and genuinely immoral behavior in such a memorable fashion that Augustine likes to use animal examples when he composes homilies in which he exhorts his auditors to behave morally. Here is an example from his *Eighty-Three Questions* 71.1:

> T4. Just as some people, zealous of acquiring such knowledge, recount of stags, that when a herd crosses over a body of water to an island for the purpose of feeding, the stags so arrange themselves that they support by turn the burden of their heads, which are heavy with the weight of their horns; and they do this in such a manner that each stag places his outstretched head on the back of the stag in front of him. And since of necessity the one preceding all the other has no support before him on which to rest his head, they are said to assume this position by turns, so that the one which preceded the others, when wearied by the weight of his head, retires behind all the others, and his place is taken by one whose head he was supporting when he was in the first place himself. Thus bearing one another's burdens by turn, they cross over the water to solid land. Solomon perhaps had this custom of the stags in mind when he said, "Let the stag of friendship . . . have converse with you," for nothing so [much] proves friendship as the bearing of a friend's burden.[1]

Does Augustine, like Thomas Nagel, suppose, in Nagel's memorable phrase, "there is something it is like to be a bat"? Or, for that matter, that there is something it is like to be a stag? I think there can be no doubt that he does. That is, I think that Augustine, like Nagel, and like most of the rest of us, supposes that mammals and birds, and perhaps other living creatures as well, have subjective experience, even when, as is the case with bats, the animal has such a different sensory apparatus from us that a bat's phenomenal world may be beyond our ability to imagine. Nagel makes that 'may' a 'must.' "So if extrapolation from our own case is involved in the idea of what it is like to be a bat," Nagel writes, "the extrapolation must be incompletable."[2]

Nagel generalizes this conclusion. He claims that "if there is conscious life elsewhere in the universe, it is likely that some of it will not be describable even in the most general experiential terms available to us." Then he adds a comment that brings us back to Augustine and the Argument from Analogy. "The problem is not confined to exotic cases, however," he writes, "for it exists between one person and another. The subjective character of the experience of a person deaf and blind from birth is not accessible to me, for example, nor presumably is mine to him. This does not prevent us each from believing that the other's experience has such a subjective character."[3]

The Argument from Analogy in Augustine is an argument for the conclusion that there are rational souls, or minds, that belong to other rational organisms, that is, in other human animals. Moreover, there are souls, even though they are not rational ones, in certain nonrational organisms, that is, in certain nonhuman animals. It does not require that we reach our conclusion about other minds and souls by building up a case for supposing that there are specifically identifiable acts or states in these other minds and souls that are like acts and states we can identify in our own mind and soul. Indeed, it seems compatible with considerable agnosticism about what exactly the subjective experience of, say, a bat, or even a dog, or a human person who has been deaf and blind from birth, really is.

In fact, Augustine expresses such skepticism in, for example, this exchange from his earliest extant dialogue, *Against the Academicians*:

T5. "Tell me instead whether the leaves of the wild olive-tree, which the goat so stubbornly desires, are bitter in themselves."

"You shameless man! The goat itself has more modesty! I don't know how they are to brute animals, but they are bitter to me." (3.11.26)

Although Augustine expresses agnosticism about how the leaves of the wild olive tree taste to the goat, he is in no doubt that they have some taste or other for the goat, that there is something it is like for the goat to taste the leaves of a wild olive tree.

I said Augustine's conclusion about other minds is compatible with "considerable agnosticism" about what the subjective experience of another minded creature might be. But surely, someone may appropriately insist, *not complete agnosticism*. We may be quite puzzled about how a dog can walk long distances on a broken leg, as if feeling no pain. But surely the yelping behavior of an injured dog contributes, indeed contributes essentially, to our assurance that a dog has real pain and hence has a phenomenal world, and is not, as Descartes tells us, a mere automaton. So even if the argument, as stated in Augustine, is too general to mention specific mental states and episodes as correlates to bodily activity, anyone who takes the argument seriously will have to rest its plausibility on some such rather specific correlations.

Here I find myself wanting to say something that may strike you as highly paradoxical. Augustine certainly does say, indeed he says it in the very passage I quoted near the beginning, that I learn what a mind is from my own case. I want to explore in a moment why he says this and what he could mean by saying it. At the same time, he does not say, nor, I think, would he want to say, that I learn what a pain is from identifying pains in myself. And the reason is that such learning, if it were to take place, would have to be learning by a sort of private ostension, and Augustine is quite as insistent as Wittgenstein that ostension is, by itself, inadequate for learning. (This is something we discussed back in chapter 4.)

Wittgenstein is, of course, quite well known for being skeptical about the efficacy of learning merely from ostension, whether "inner" or "outer." Here is a famous passage that illustrates the point:

> T6. The definition of the number two, "That is called 'two'" – pointing to two nuts – is perfectly exact, – But how can two be defined like that? The person one gives the definition to doesn't know what one wants to call "two"; he will suppose that "two" is the name given to *this* group of nuts! – He *may* suppose this; but perhaps he does not. He might make the opposite mistake; when I want to assign a name to this group of nuts, he might understand it as a numeral. And he might equally well take the name of a person, of which I give an ostensive definition, as that of a colour, of a race, or even of a point of the compass. That is to say: an ostensive definition can be variously interpreted in *every* case.[4]

As it turns out, Augustine is equally skeptical of the efficacy of ostensive learning. No doubt the best place to look for evidence of Augustine's skepticism about ostensive learning, that is, learning by having examples pointed out or displayed to the learner, is his early dialogue *The Teacher*, which we discussed in chapter 4. Here is the passage in which Augustine asks whether one can demonstrate by example what the word 'walking' means, if one is already walking:

T7. Augustine: Now do this: tell me – if I were completely ignorant of the meaning of the word ['walking'] and were to ask you what walking is while you were walking, how would you teach me?
Adeodatus: I would do it a little bit more quickly, so that after your question you would be prompted by something novel [in my behavior], and yet nothing would take place other than what was to be shown.
Augustine: Don't you know that *walking* is one thing and *hurrying* another? . . . We speak of 'hurrying' in writing and in reading and in countless other matters. (3.6)

Adeodatus later returns to this example of walking:

T8. Adeodatus: For example, if anyone should ask me what it is to walk while I was resting or doing something else, as was said, and I should attempt to teach him what he asked about without a sign, by immediately walking, how shall I guard against his thinking that it's just the amount of walking I have done? He'll be mistaken if he thinks this. He'll think that anyone who walks farther than I have, or not as far, hasn't walked at all. (10.29)

As we saw in chapter 4, Augustine moves later on to the example of bird-catching. He asks Adeodatus whether someone could be shown what bird-catching is by demonstrating the practice. Adeodatus is skeptical. "I'm afraid that everything here is like what I said about the man who asks what it is to walk." Augustine tries to reassure him, "It's easy to get rid of your worry," he replies:

T9. I add that he's so intelligent that he recognizes the kind of craft as a whole on the basis of what he has seen. It's surely enough for the matter at hand that some men can be taught about some things, even if not all, without a sign. (10.32)

I should explain that the discussion of whether one can teach another what walking is, or what bird-catching is, "without a sign," is primarily a discussion of whether it can be done without using words, that is, by simply pointing out examples, or by demonstrating an activity or practice. Later in *The Teacher* Augustine argues that there really is no teaching with signs either, that is, there is no ostensive teaching of the meaning of words by using signs. One has to learn for oneself, by consulting the "inner teacher." This is the so-called "Doctrine of Illumination" in Augustine. It presupposes that Platonic-style ideas are immediately available to each of us. Ostension or discussion in language can prompt us to consult the "inner teacher" and locate *walking* or *bird-catching* either as themselves Platonic ideas or as complexes made up of Platonic ideas.

Actually it is not quite accurate to say that Augustine's Doctrine of Illumination or his idea of "the inner teacher" is Platonic, since Augustine himself tried to distinguish his views from Plato's. In Book 12 of *On the Trinity*, after making a reference to Plato's story in his dialogue *Meno*, in which the slave-boy is able to figure out for himself how to construct a square with an area twice that of a given square, Augustine says this, with, I think, a touch of humor:

> T10. Yet if this were a recollecting of things previously known, then certainly everyone, or almost everyone, would be unable to do the same thing if questioned in this manner. For not all have been geometricians in their previous life, since there are so few of them in the human race that one can hardly be found. (12.15.24)

Augustine continues, quite seriously now:

> T11. But we ought rather to believe that the nature of the intellectual mind is so formed as to see those things which, according to the disposition of the Creator, are subjoined to intelligible things in the natural order, in a sort of incorporeal light of its own kind, as the eye of the flesh sees the things that lie about it in this corporeal light, of which light it is made to be receptive and to which it is adapted. (12.15.24)

Augustine goes on to say that sensible things, including, presumably colors, or bodily actions such as walking, or bird-catching, must be observed with our senses, though, as we have seen, he thinks that we will not be able to pick out what a color is, or what walking or bird-catching is, without the illumination of the "inner teacher."

With these views about the ineffectiveness of ostensive teaching and learning, it would be inappropriate for Augustine to assume that we can learn what a pain is, or what anxiety is, or what thinking about Vienna is (Augustine's stock case is thinking about Alexandria, which is a city he seems to have fantasized about, though he never visited it) by a kind of inner ostension. To be sure, Augustine does not, like Wittgenstein, express worries about what would be the difference between getting a re-identification of a pain right and only seeming to do so. But he already has sufficient worries about the efficacy of ostensive learning to make it quite inappropriate for him to think one could teach oneself what pain is.

Thus one would not expect Augustine to develop a "bottom-up" argument for other minds (there must be pain, anxiety, desire, thoughts about Alexandria, etc. in that body over there; so it has a mind). And, in fact, we find no such thing. Indeed, it is a "top-down" argument – from a whole repertoire of bodily movements that resemble movements in my body that I notice my mind bringing about, to the conclusion that there must be a mind in that other body that brings about that repertoire of movements. This argument is, I think, quite compatible with considerable agnosticism about the phenomenal character of that other organism's inner life, agnosticism about what it is actually like to be that bat or other human being.

Yet the argument does depend on the assumption that I can know what a mind is from my own case. And Augustine insists on this assumption: "We can also know what a mind [*animus*] is by considering our own," he writes, "for we have a mind" (*On the Trinity* 8.6.9). This is clearly reasoning from one's own case, even if it is not reasoning from specific mental acts or states to the attribution of the same, or the same type of, mental act or state to another. Why is Augustine not skeptical about my ability to pick out my own mind?

The answer is, as large sections of the *On the Trinity* try to impress on us, that the mind is by nature an entity that is immediately present to itself. It does not need to pick itself out. In fact, Augustine is puzzled about what it could possibly pick itself out *from*. In Nagel's language, if there is something it is like to be the sort of entity I am, then I cannot help but know what it is. The activities and passivities of my mind constitute what it is like to be the kind of thing I am. My thoughts, my feelings, my dreams, my daydreams, my desires, my fears – all these help make up what it is like to be my kind of thing.

As we noted in the last chapter, Augustine tries to bring out the immediate availability of the mind to itself by puzzling over the classical Greek admonition 'Know thyself!':

> T12. How can the mind come into the mind, as though it were possible for the mind not to be in the mind? Add to this, that if a part has been found, then the mind does not seek itself as a whole, but yet it does seek itself as a whole. Therefore, it is present to itself as a whole, and there is nothing further to be sought. For nothing is wanting to the mind that seeks; only the object that is sought is wanting. Since it, therefore, seeks itself as a whole, nothing of itself is wanting to it. (*On the Trinity* 10.4.6)

Augustine concludes that the command 'Know thyself!' must not be an admonition to the mind to seek out something of itself that it does not yet know, there being no such thing. Rather, he says, this admonition must be a command to the soul to "consider itself and live according to its nature, namely, under Him [i.e., God] to whom it must be brought into subjection." He adds that the mind "does many things through evil desires, as though it had forgotten itself" (10.5.7). This forgetfulness Augustine conceives as a sort of "turning away" from the mind's true nature, but not a real ignorance of what it is.

What might a Wittgensteinian critic say to the argument I have reconstructed from Augustine? I would anticipate two lines of attack. First,

I would expect the critic to say that the vague reference to behavior routines, or more sanitarily, movement routines, cannot be persuasive. We need to attribute pain to the writhing bat, or thinking that the ball is behind the couch to the infant child who is playing hide-and-seek, to give the Argument from Analogy any purchase at all.

I myself feel torn on this question. On the one hand, our confidence that the stroke victim, or the Alzheimer's patient, has a mind, does indeed seem to hang to some extent on identifiable behavior routines. But, on the other hand, I do not think I have any good idea at all of what it is like *to be* a stroke victim, or *to be* a patient suffering from Alzheimer's disease. However, my agnosticism about what it is like to be an Alzheimer patient in no way shakes my confidence that there *is* something it is like to be such a person – that Alzheimer patients do have minds. And the same is true for bats.

The other thing I would expect a Wittgensteinian critic to say is that it is a mistake to suppose we attribute a mind to another being on the basis of an argument. This response finds support from Wittgenstein's famous saying in the *Investigations*:

> T13. My attitude towards him is an attitude towards a soul. I am not of the opinion that he has a soul.[5]

If I understand this dark saying, it implies that I do not so much reason to the conclusion that x has a soul as develop an attitude of empathy, or resentment, or concern, or whatever, towards another soul.

I myself feel rather ambivalent about this response as well. In becoming a vegetarian I did not so much change my opinions about steers and chickens as I did change my attitude towards them. However, it is not as though reasoning played no role at all. Thus it was important to me to be given evidence that all birds and all mammals dream. There is not similar evidence, I understand, for dreaming in amphibians, fish, or lower animals. I reasoned that any organism that dreams very likely has subjective experience of some sort, perhaps not totally unlike mine. Thinking about that, I found myself not wanting to eat the dreamers. Reasoning affected my attitudes.

Is there then nothing it is like to be a frog, or a lobster, since they, apparently, do not dream (or, more cautiously, since we do not have similar reason to think that they dream.)? I do not know. But that seems to me a question that can be discussed. It is reasonable, I think, to have an opinion about it. And relevant to forming such an opinion is, I think, not only the neurophysiology of such organisms, but also the behavior patterns that might offer analogies to patterns in higher animals.

In some passages, Wittgenstein himself seems to support the search for analogies to back up the attribution of "soul" to other creatures. Thus he tells us that "only of a living human being and what resembles (behaves like) a living human being can one say: it has sensations; it sees; is blind; hears; is deaf; is conscious or unconscious" (281). And again, "Only of what behaves like a human being can one say that it *has* pains" (283). And further, "We say only of a human being and what is like one that it thinks" (360).

Two things strike me as especially important about those last remarks of Wittgenstein. First of all, Wittgenstein's idea of supposing that only what is *like* a human being thinks, and only what *behaves* like one has pains, makes clear that Wittgenstein is using some analogical thinking of his own. The second thing is, in the first quote he says that only of what behaves like a human being *can* one say that it has pains. He might have contented himself with a psychological or social observation and remarked that only of such beings *are we inclined* to say that they have pains. But by saying only of such beings *can* we say that they have pains he seems to be introducing a question about what it is legitimate to say, or what one could be justified in saying. And that seems to mean that the perceived analogy he is insisting on is not merely efficacious in getting us to talk empathetically about those creatures, but that it is also the required basis for the *legitimate* attribution of pain or other mental states or acts to those beings. And that seems to me to be so close to the very general Argument from Analogy for Other Minds which we find in Augustine that I am no longer confident Wittgenstein should be viewed as a critic of this general argument.

In fact, Wittgenstein even inches a little closer, as in this immediately following passage:

T14. Look at a stone and imagine it having sensations. – One says to one-self: How could one so much as get the idea of ascribing a *sensation* to a *thing*? One might as well ascribe it to a number! – And now look at a wrig-gling fly and at once these difficulties vanish and pain seems able to get a foothold here (*der Schmerz scheint hier* angreifen *zu können*) . . .[6]

Admittedly, Wittgenstein does not explain why the wriggling of the fly gives the attribution of sensation a foothold, or what more would be required to give such attribution a solid foundation. But he has invited us to think about that question, even if only somewhat coyly. It would be natural to answer the question with some form of the Argument from Analogy for Other Minds.

So what, again, is the Wittgensteinian objection to the Argument from Analogy for Other Minds supposed to be? Is it just a rejection of the idea that one could possibly learn from one's own case by "private" intro-spection what a pain is, or what the feeling of anxiety is and then, on the basis of similarities in the behavior of bodies other than one's own, attribute *that same feeling* to another organism? If so, there may not be as much to separate Augustine from Wittgenstein as we had first thought. As we have seen, Augustine is, in his way, as skeptical about the efficacy of ostensive learning as Wittgenstein is. But, whereas Augustine responds to this skepticism with a close relative of Platonic innatism, Wittgenstein responds with an appeal to "outer criteria" for the ascription of "inner episodes" and, more generally, to language games and to forms of life.

further reading

Gareth B. Matthews, "Descartes and the problem of other minds," in Amelie O. Rorty (ed.), *Essays on Descartes's Meditations*. Berkeley: University of California Press, 1986, pp. 141–51. In this essay I reflect on the absence of an argument for other minds in Descartes.

notes

1 Augustine, *Eighty-Three Different Questions*, tr. D. L. Mosher (Washington, DC: Catholic University of America Press, 1982).
2 Thomas Nagel, "What is it like to be a bat?" *Philosophical Review* 83 (1974): 439.
3 Ibid., p. 440.
4 Ludwig Wittgenstein, *Philosophical Investigations*, tr. G. E. M. Anscombe (Oxford: Blackwell, 1967), p. 28.
5 Ibid., pt. II, iv, p. 178.
6 Ibid., p. 284.

philosophical dream problems

One who does philosophy from a first-person point of view, as Augustine does, may have to face one or more of three different dream problems. The first I call the *Epistemological Dream Problem*: How do I know whether I am *now* dreaming? The second I call the *Metaphysical Dream Problem*: How do I know whether all life is my dream? And the third I call the *Moral Dream Problem*: Can I be immoral by doing something immoral in my dream?

the epistemological dream problem

Of the three dream problems, the Epistemological Dream Problem seems to have had the longest history. It is raised in Plato's dialogue *Theaetetus* at 158bc:

SOCRATES: There's a question you must often have heard people ask – the question what evidence we could offer if we were asked whether in the present instance, at this moment, we are asleep and dreaming all our thoughts, or awake and talking to each other in real life.
THEAETETUS: Yes, Socrates, it certainly is difficult to find the proof we want here. The two states seem to correspond in all their characteristics. There is nothing to prevent us from thinking when we are asleep that we are having the very same discussion that we have just had. And when we dream that we are telling the story of a dream, there is an extraordinary likeness between the two experiences.[1]

Plato has Socrates raise this question as part of his examination of the suggestion that knowledge is perception. In his consideration of the question he goes on to say that, since our dreaming periods are equal in length to our waking periods, we have no good reason to give special weight to the beliefs of our waking periods. But to make that point is already to move away from the pure Epistemological Dream Problem and to suppose we have a vantage point from which we can view both our remembered dream lives and our remembered waking lives in the full confidence that we are not, as we view these two lives, having a dream.

Thus, although Plato poses the Epistemological Dream Problem, he does not take it very seriously. Assuming that judgments formed in dreams are epistemologically suspect (which is, I think, a plausible assumption), what Plato fails to take seriously is that the Epistemological Dream Problem might undermine all our judgments. Thus, if for no *now* can I know I am not *now* dreaming, then every judgment I make is under suspicion of being illusory.

Aristotle seems to have seen the threat of the Epistemological Dream Problem more clearly. He writes in *Metaphysics* 4, 1011a3–13:

> Some . . . are perplexed because they want to know who will judge who is healthy, and in general on each subject [who is to say] who will judge it correctly. Such perplexities are similar to the perplexing question 'Are we now asleep or awake?' and they all have the same force. For those who pose them ask for an argument for everything; for they seek a principle, and they seek to get it through demonstration . . . the trouble is just as we have stated: for they seek an argument for something for which there is no argument, for a principle of demonstration is not a demonstration.[2]

Aristotle's point about principles of demonstration seems to be this. Suppose we have this simple *modus ponens* argument:

(1) Koko is a primate.
(2) If Koko is a primate, then Koko is a mammal. Therefore,
(3) Koko is a mammal.

Suppose someone asks what makes (3) follow from (1) and (2). We might reply that it follows by the *principle of modus ponens*. But, of course we have not proved *modus ponens* by our argument from (1) and (2) to (3). We have appealed to this law of logic to prove (3) from (1) and (2). We could try to prove *modus ponens* by appeal to some other law of logic. But now we could be off on an indefinite regress, since that other "principle of demonstration" would not have been proved either.

Aristotle seems to think that something similar is true of the Epistemological Dream Problem. Suppose I demand a reliable sign that I am now awake before I consider myself justified in accepting some judgment I am making. The sign could be, say, the brightness and coherence of my experience. And suppose that I have the experience of making some judgment and I check to see whether it is bright and coherent. The skeptic can ask how I know that I am not just dreaming that I am checking to see that it is bright and coherent. It seems I would need a reliable sign that my application of the brightness-and-coherence test was not itself a dream. And so, again, we would be off on an indefinite regress. Aristotle's response to the Epistemological Dream Problem is to ignore it, on the grounds that, since there could be no satisfactory answer to it, it is misconceived.

Unlike Plato, Augustine takes the threat of the Epistemological Dream Problem seriously. And unlike Aristotle, he does not deliberately choose to ignore it. Instead, he seeks to limit the damage it threatens. As we saw in chapter 5, his *cogito* reasoning is aimed at showing that I can know certain things whether or not I am dreaming. Thus, whether or not I am dreaming, I can know, he argues, that I exist, that I know I exist, and that I am glad to exist and to know that I do. Here is a passage from *On the Trinity*, where the knowledge claim is not 'I know that I exist,' but rather 'I know that I am alive':

T1. It is an inner knowledge by which we know that we live, where not even the Academician can say: "Perhaps you are sleeping, and you do not know, and you see in dreams." For who does not know that things seen by those who are asleep are very similar to things seen by those who are awake? But he who is certain about the knowledge of his own life does not say in it, "I know that I am awake," but "I know that I live"; whether he, therefore, sleeps, or whether he is awake, he lives. He cannot be deceived in his knowledge of this even by dreams. (15.12.21)

Augustine's response to the Epistemological Dream Problem is something we can call "the Illusion Response." The idea behind the Illusion Response is this. In our waking life, as well as when we dream, when we are drunken, and when we are mad, what we perceive, or think we perceive, may be only an illusion. While we are under an illusion, we may not realize that this is so. But eventually we are usually able to sort things out and determine whether what we once thought was the case was really only an illusion.

Yet even when we are under an illusion and fail to realize that we are under an illusion, there may be some things that we know because they seem to us to be so and we cannot be mistaken about them. Thus we may know that we exist, that we are alive, and that $2 + 2 = 4$, even if we are dreaming. The illusions of dreams may be more extensive than, say, the illusion that parallel tracks meet at the horizon. But their extensiveness does not change their character as illusions, nor does it rule out the possibility that there are some things we know, whether we are dreaming or awake.

Here, in his early treatise *On the Immortality of the Soul* is Augustine's fullest statement of what I am calling the "Illusion Response" to the Epistemological Dream Problem:

T2. If, for instance, someone during a dream has appeared to himself to be engaged in a discussion and, pursuing true principles, has learned something in this discussion, then these true principles also remain the same and unchangeable after his awakening. Yet, other circumstances may be found [to be] untrue, such as the place of the discussion, or the person with whom he seemed to have the discussion, and – as far as their sound is concerned – even the words seemingly used in the discussion, and other things of such kind as are to be perceived, or acted upon, through the senses by awakened persons. Yet these things pass away and in no way reach the level of everlasting presence of true principles. From this one may conclude that, through a bodily change such as sleep, the soul's use of the same body can be reduced, but not the soul's proper life. (14.23)

Just as in waking life one's judgment may be impaired without one's realizing that it is impaired, so one's judgment in sleep may be impaired without one's realizing it. I may think I am in Carthage, when I am not. I may think I am speaking to my mother, when I am not. Still, there are things I can know even in a dream. For example, I can know that I exist and that the whole is greater than any proper part. I can know these things if they seem to me to be the case and I cannot be mistaken in thinking them. Eventually I will be able to recognize the illusions for what they were. The knowledge will stand.

the metaphysical dream problem

The Metaphysical Dream Problem is, in effect, the challenge of solipsism. If all life were my dream, then the only things that exist would be me and my dream contents, that is, my thoughts and experiences.

No important philosopher has ever *claimed* to be a solipsist. What could be the point of making such a claim? And to whom could one make it? The only reason to take the Metaphysical Dream Problem seriously is to ask whether I have a rational justification for believing there is a world independent of me, my thoughts, and experiences.

Descartes takes this problem seriously. Having proved, to his satisfaction, that God exists and is perfectly good, Descartes argues, in *Meditation* 6, that there must be a physical world, more or less similar to his representation of it. If there were not, he maintains, there would be no way for him to free himself from the great illusion of there being such a world. And God would then be a great deceiver in letting him suffer under this illusion. Moreover, as he thinks he has proved, God is no deceiver.

Augustine might have been expected to confront the Metaphysical Dream Problem in Book 3 of his *Against the Academicians*. Asked if he knows that the world exists, he suggests considering whatever appears to him "the world." Even if he does not know that an independent physical world exists, he does know that there is what he is calling "the world," that is, the world of his own thoughts and impressions, his phenomenal world. That move sets the stage for the Metaphysical Dream Problem. But Augustine never discusses the problem. As I pointed out in chapter 3, we never find him grappling with "the Problem of the External World."

the moral dream problem

Plato was perhaps the first philosopher to ask about the morality of what we do in our dreams. Socrates is made to say in Book 9 of Plato's *Republic*:

> Some of our unnecessary pleasures and desires seem to me to be lawless. They are probably present in everyone, but they are held in check by the laws and by the better desires in alliance with reason. In a few people, they have been eliminated entirely or only a few weak ones remain, while in others they are stronger and more numerous. (571bc)

Glaucon wants to know what desires Socrates has in mind. So Socrates explains:

> Those that are awakened in sleep, when the rest of the soul – the rational, gentle, and ruling part – slumbers. Then the beastly and savage part, full of food and drink, casts off sleep and seeks to find a way to gratify itself. You know that there is nothing it won't dare to do at such a time, free of all control by shame or reason. It doesn't shrink from trying to have sex with a mother, as it supposes, or with anyone else at all, whether man, god, or beast. It will commit any foul murder, and there is no food it refuses to eat. In a word, it omits no act of folly or shamelessness. (571cd)

In a way Socrates here identifies himself with his dream self and in a way he distinguishes himself from his dream self. He has already in Book 4 of the *Republic* divided the soul or self into three parts: the appetitive, the spirited, and the rational. Here he makes the appetitive part the agent in the revelries of shameful dreams, while the rational part sleeps. But is it not still he who enjoys unlawful sex and unbridled pleasures, even if part of himself, the rational and law-abiding part, is asleep and out of the picture? Plato does not have his character Socrates actually say anything much like what St. Paul says in his letter to the Romans, "It is no longer I that do it, but sin which dwells within me" (Romans 7:20). But it seems clear that Socrates wants to identify himself with his rational self, the self that is asleep during one's dreams.

Instead of worrying about whether he is his dream self, Socrates offers some practical advice on how to put one's lustful self to sleep when one's reason is about to doze off:

> I suppose that someone who is healthy and moderate with himself goes to sleep only after having done the following: First, he rouses his rational part and feasts it on fine arguments and speculations; second, he neither starves nor feasts his appetites, so that they will slumber and not disturb his best part with either their pleasure or their pain, but they'll leave it alone, pure and by itself, to look for something – it knows not what – and try to perceive it, whether it is past, present, or future; third, he soothes his spirited part in the same way, for example, by not falling asleep with his spirit still aroused after an outburst of anger. And when he has quieted these two parts and aroused the third, in which reason resides, and so takes his rest, you know that it is then that he best grasps the truth and that the visions that appear in his dreams are least lawless. (571d–572b)

Plato thus seems to view the appetitive self as a constant companion, someone we are inseparably tied to, in this life anyway. The rational self, the "real me," is thus not responsible for what my appetitive self does in dreams *by actually being that self*. Still, it is responsible for taming the appetitive self properly before "the real me" abandons it and goes to sleep.

Augustine has great difficulty distinguishing himself from his dream self, as this fascinating passage from Book 10 of his *Confessions* makes clear:

> T3. You commanded me without question to abstain "from the lust of the flesh and the lust of the eyes and the ambition of the secular world" (1 *John* 2:16). You commanded me to abstain from sleeping with a girl-friend and, in regard to marriage itself, you advised me to adopt a better way of life than you have allowed (1 *Corinthians* 7:38). And because you granted me strength, this was done even before I became a dispenser of your sacrament. But in my memory of which I have spoken at length, there still live images of acts which were fixed there by my sexual habit. These images attack me. While I am awake they have no force, but in sleep they not only arouse pleasure but even elicit consent, and are very like the actual act. The illusory image within the soul has such force upon my flesh that false dreams have an effect on me when asleep, which the reality could not have when I am awake. During this time of sleep surely it is my true self, Lord my God? Yet how great a difference between myself at the time when I am asleep and myself when I return to the waking state. Where then is reason which, when wide-awake, resists such suggestive thoughts, and would remain unmoved if the actual reality were to be presented to it? Surely reason does not shut down as the eyes close. It can hardly fall asleep with the bodily senses. For if that were so, how could it come about that often in

sleep we resist and, mindful of our avowed commitment and adhering to it with strict chastity, we give no assent to such seductions? Yet there is a difference so great that, when it happens otherwise than we would wish, when we wake up we return to peace in our conscience. From the wide gulf between the occurrences and our will, we discover that we did not actively do what, to our regret, has somehow been done in us. (10.30.41)

Although there are other statements of the Moral Dream Problem in Augustine, for example, *The Literal Meaning of Genesis* 12.15.31, T3 is the most extensive and the most tortured one. Clearly Augustine finds his dreams of having sex troubling and somehow unfair testimony to his sexual appetite.

Although it seems to have been primarily, if not solely, the sexual acts in his dreams that Augustine found troubling, the Moral Dream Problem he raises is perfectly general. Certainly I have myself dreamt I performed deeds that I found troubling when I recalled them upon awakening. I suspect that my readers have as well. Am I morally responsible for those acts of my dream self?

There seem to be three distinct ways one might try to get out of responsibility for one's dream self:

(1) *I could say that my dream self is not really me.* In fact, there is already a problem about identifying my dream self, even before we raise a question about moral responsibility. Sometimes I think of myself as a character I observe in my dream. It is as if I am viewing myself in a movie. At other times I think of my dream self as the observer of my dream. In those cases I may make comments in the dream about what is happening, but I do not see myself in the dream. But whether my dream self is a character in my dream or simply the observer of my dream, or perhaps sometimes one and sometimes the other, I might try insisting that this dream self is not really me. If the dream self is not really me, then I am not directly responsible for the acts or thoughts of my dream self, since I am not the person who performs those acts or has those thoughts.

(2) *I can insist that what happens in my dreams is not anything that really happens, unless by mere coincidence.* Of course, I might dream that something is happening when, by coincidence, that very thing happens in real life. However, it is only real-life deeds or thoughts for which I am morally responsible.

(3) *I can insist that I am morally responsible only for what is within my power to refrain from doing. What I do in my dreams is not anything that is within my power to refrain from doing.*

Is any one of these responses open to Augustine? What about (1)? Can Augustine consistently deny that he is his dream self?

I think the answer is 'No.' As we saw in our discussion of Augustine's response to the Epistemological Dream Problem, he treats dreams as illusions, illusions that one has when one is asleep. If I go into a virtual reality machine and have the illusion that I have knocked out the boxer who seems to be standing in front of me, I will be the very person I have the illusion has knocked out the boxer. Similarly, if I dream that I knock out a boxer, I am the very one who knocks out the boxer in my dream.

In his book *On the Soul and Its Origins* Augustine is quite explicit on this very point:

T4. For in dreams, when we suffer anything harsh and troublesome, we are, of course, still ourselves . . . (4.17.25)

I may think thoughts in a fit of anger, or in a drunken state, that I later wish I had not thought. Those thoughts may or may not reflect my true beliefs. But they are undoubtedly my thoughts, even if the context in which I had them was a fit of anger, or a drunken state. So, given Augustine's Illusion Response to the Epistemological Dream Problem, he must acknowledge that the thoughts my dream self has are my very own thoughts. They are mine even though the context in which I have them is illusory.

What about (2)? Can Augustine consistently maintain that nothing really happens when I dream that such-and-such an event has taken place?

Like the rest of us, Augustine would want to say that, when I fall off a cliff in my dream, it is not really the case that I have fallen off a cliff. What he is *not* free to say is that, when I have, in a dream, the thought that I hate my neighbor, I have not had the thought that I hate my neighbor. As he says in T2, "through a bodily change such as sleep, the soul's use of the same body can be reduced, but not the soul's proper life."

This point takes on weighty significance when we realize that Augustine is an "intentionalist" in ethics. I do something morally wrong, he thinks, if (1) a wrongful or sinful action suggests itself to me, (2) I take pleasure in the suggestion, and, finally, (3) I consent to perform the action suggested. According to Augustine, I sin, that is, I do something morally wrong, simply by consenting to the wrongful suggestion, even if I never carry out the action I have "consented" to perform.[3]

I sin and commit a moral wrong, according to Augustine, when I consent to have sex with someone to whom I am not married. Since the thoughts, including the mental acts of consent performed by my dream self, are my thoughts, my consents, I sin, or commit a moral wrong, in my dream by consenting to commit adultery in that dream, even if I am completely chaste in my waking life.

So response (2) is not open to Augustine. What about response (3)? Can I not plead that what I do or think in my dreams is not anything within my power?

What we have to say about this "way out" is rather complicated. Augustine devoted much energy and effort to putting down what is called the "Pelagian heresy." In fact, it was Augustine, more than anyone else, who defined Pelagianism as a heresy.

Pleagius was a Christian monk, a contemporary of Augustine's, who taught that we can be righteous by our own unassisted efforts. Augustine insisted that we can do nothing good by our own power, without the grace of God.

The Pelagian idea can be put in the slogan "'Ought' implies 'can'," which is a motto many philosophers today associate with the great German philosopher, Immanuel Kant. Thus:

(a) If S ought to do A, then S can do A.

In effect, Augustine's doctrine of Divine grace requires us to ask for a clarification of (a). Does it mean this, he wants to know?

(b) If S ought to do A, then S can do A, quite independently of the gratuitous assistance (i.e., the grace) of God?

Or does it mean this?

(c) If S ought to do A, then S can do A, though perhaps only with the gratuitous assistance (i.e., the grace) of God.

Not surprisingly, Augustine rejects (b). It is, for him, an expression of the Pelagian heresy. But he accepts (c).

Now we need to disambiguate (3), and the idea that what I do in my dreams is not anything that is within my power. Does it mean this?

(3a) What I do in my dreams is not anything that is within my power to refrain from doing, independently of the grace of God.

Or does it mean this?

(3b) What I do in my dreams is not anything it is within my power to refrain from doing, even with the grace of God.

(3a) is hardly available to Augustine. He cannot use it as a way of getting himself off the hook. On his view there is nothing worthwhile that he can do unassisted by the grace of God. So his inability to refrain, unassisted by the grace of God, from sinning in his dreams does not mark off this case from any other case of being unable to refrain from sinning unassisted by the grace of God.

As for (3b), this is something he will reject out of hand. In fact, he rejects it in the very next section:

T5. It cannot be the case, almighty God, that your hand is not enough to cure all the sickness of my soul and, by a more abundant outflow of your grace, to extinguish the lascivious impulses of my sleep. You will more and more increase your gifts in me, Lord, so that my soul, rid of the glue of lust, may follow me to you, so that it is not in rebellion against itself, and so that even in dreams it not only does not commit those disgraceful and corrupt acts in which sensual images provoke carnal emissions, but also does not even consent to them. (10.30.42)

Still, Augustine does say in T3, "Yet there is a difference so great [between consent in dreams and consent when awake] that, when it happens otherwise than we would wish [i.e., when we consent to a sinful act in our dreams], when we wake up we return to peace in our conscience." But this is just so much whistling in the dark. Augustine makes clear by the way he brings up the moral dream problem that he does not awaken to peace in his conscience. No doubt his nocturnal emissions are an obvious reminder that he has been unchaste in his dream. Moreover, he does not understand how it can be that he is not responsible for consenting in his dream to what he considers sinful. But that hardly means he "returns to peace" in his conscience when he wakes up. Rather he wakes up to a nagging worry. "It cannot be the case, almighty God," he writes, "that your hand is not strong enough to cure all the sickness of my soul and, by a more abundant outflow of your grace, to extinguish the lascivious impulses of my sleep" (10.40.32). Implicit is the nagging question "But then why don't you extinguish the lascivious impulses of my sleep?"

Those of us who are not committed to Augustine's Illusion Response to the Epistemological Dream Problem may think we can be content with the first way of getting out of moral responsibility for what we do, or consent to do, in our dreams: we are not our dream selves. But we should not be too easy on ourselves. Consider Freud's response to the Moral Dream Problem.

Freud distinguishes between the *manifest* content of a dream and its *latent* content. The manifest content is the story one is able to tell on waking, without seeking any interpretation of the dream's significance. According to the manifest content I may be the observer of what happened in the dream or I may be one of the actors in the dream. The latent content is given in the proper interpretation of the dream, perhaps something I come to understand only after appropriate psychoanalysis.

With this distinction between manifest content and latent content, we can see that we cannot assume that my dream self, whether dream observer or dream participant, is simply me. It may be some kind of projection. Still, Freud is quite stern about getting us to accept moral responsibility for our dreams. In an addendum to his *Interpretation of Dreams* titled "Moral responsibility for the content of dreams" he writes:

> If I seek to classify the impulses that are present in me according to social standards into good and bad, I must assume responsibility for both sorts; and if, in defense, I say that what is unknown, unconscious and repressed in me is not my "ego," then I shall not be basing my position upon psychoanalysis, I shall not have accepted its conclusions and I shall perhaps be taught better by the criticisms of my fellow men, by the disturbances in my actions and by the confusion of my feelings. I shall perhaps learn that what I am repudiating not only "is" in me but sometimes "acts" from out of me as well.[4]

further reading
Ishtiyaque Haji, "On being morally responsible in a dream," in Gareth B. Matthews (ed.), *The Augustinian Tradition*. Berkeley: University of California Press, 1999, pp. 166–82. Haji offers thoughtful reflections on the moral dream problem and some of the implications of that problem.

notes
1 Plato, *Theaetetus*, tr. M. J. Levett (Indianapolis: Hackett, 1999).
2 Aristotle, *Metaphysics, Books Γ, Δ, and E*, tr. C. Kirwan (Oxford: Clarendon Press, 1971).
3 See Augustine's *The Lord's Sermon on the Mount* 1.12.33–4.
4 Sigmund Freud, *Collected Papers*, tr. J. Strachey (New York: Basic Books, 1959), 5:154–7.

time and creation

Augustine takes the first verse of the first chapter of Genesis, "In the beginning God made heaven and earth," to entail, not only that God created all temporal or mutable things, but also that God created time itself. Addressing God in his *Confessions*, Augustine writes:

> T1. You have made time itself. Time could not elapse before you made time. (11.13.15)

On a natural reading of T1, it entails this:

(A) There was a first time.

We might take (A) to entail something about the periods of time just before the first time, namely, that there was no time then. But that alleged entailment is incoherent, as Augustine is well aware. So, if (A) makes any sense at all, it cannot entail anything about times before the first time.

In fact, Augustine conjoins (A) with this statement:

(B) Time has existed for all time.

He reasons this way:

> T2. For if time has not existed for all time, it would follow that there was a time when there was no time. And [even] the most complete fool would not say that! (*City of God* 12.16)

So the careful thinker who accepts (A) might understand it to mean this:

(A*) There was a time, *t*, such that there was no time before *t*.

Indeed Augustine himself seems to understand (A) to mean the same thing as (A*).

One question (A*) raises is this:

(Q) What brought about the beginning of time?

In asking (Q) we might be asking for the agent or agents responsible for the beginning of time, or we might be trying to determine in some informative and so nontrivial way what conditions were both necessary and sufficient for there to be time. Thus we can divide (Q) into these two questions:

(Q1) What agent or agents brought it about that time began?
(Q2) What conditions were necessary and sufficient for there to be time?

Augustine's answer to (Q1) is, of course, 'God.' His answer to (Q2) is 'change and movement.' But to make these answers at all plausible he must suppose that God's act of creation was not preceded by anything, say, by God's deliberation about whether to create a temporal world, or even by a period of rest before the bodies moved so as to produce time. He writes:

> T3. . . . there can be no doubt that the world was not created *in* time but *with* time. An event in time happens after one time and before another, after the past and before the future. But at the time of creation there could have been no past, because there was nothing created to provide the change and movement which is the condition of time. (*City of God* 11.6)

To say that the world was not created *in* time means, I take it, that God's act of creation was not itself a temporal event. Thus, according to Augustine, God did not first deliberate and decide to create the world and then create it. Nor did he first create objects and then set them in motion. God's act of creation is an *eternal* act in the sense of being a nontemporal act. And the objects he created to initiate time must have been created in a state of motion, or change.

The idea of God's act of creation being itself a nontemporal act opens up a way of responding to the old Parmenidean worry about how anything could come to be from nothing. Parmenides asked, rhetorically, for he thought the idea of a beginning of existence from nothing absurd, "What necessity would have stirred it up to grow later rather than earlier, beginning from nothing?"[1] The Augustinian reply is that no cause was required to bring the world into existence at t, rather than at t', since there was no time before God created the world *with time*.

Augustine himself links the Parmenidean question about time (What could have brought about the beginning of the world at one time rather than another?) to a parallel question about space: Why should the world have been created here rather than in some other place? He writes:

T4. . . . the question, "Why at this time and not previously?" is on the same footing as "Why in this place rather than that?" For if they imagine that there were infinite stretches of time before the world existed, an infinity in which they cannot conceive of God's being inactive, they will, on the same showing, imagine infinite stretches of space; and if anywhere in that infinity, it will follow that they are compelled to share the Epicurean fantasy of innumerable worlds. (*City of God* 11.5)

Without the world, in Augustine's view, there would be neither time nor space. Thus the questions 'Why then?' and 'Why here?' are both inappropriate, and for roughly the same reason.

In Book 12 of the *City of God* Augustine complicates his account of the creation story somewhat by introducing a distinction between *ordered*, or *measured*, time and *unordered*, or *unmeasured*, time. Writing about the angels, he has this to say:

T5. They have existed for all time: so much so that they were created before all measured time, if we accept it that measured time began with the creation of the sky, and they existed before that. But time, we suppose, did not begin with the sky, but existed before it; though not indeed in hours, days, months, and years. For these measurements of temporal spaces, which are by usage properly called "times", evidently took their beginning from the motion of the stars; hence God said, in creating them, "Let them serve for signs and times and days and years." Time, we suppose, existed before this in some changing movement, in which there was succession of before and after, in which everything could not be simultaneous. If then before the creation of the sky there was something of this sort in the angelic motions, and therefore time already existed and the angels moved in time from the moment of their creation, even so they have existed for all time, seeing that time began whey they began. (*City of God* 12.16)

Thus, according to Augustine, time really began with the creation of the angels, who were, presumably, in motion from the moment of their creation. But the motion of the angels produced only unmeasured time. Measured time did not come into being until the (moving) heavenly bodies were created. Thus there was unmeasured time before there was measured time.

To judge by Augustine's comments in his much earlier work the *Unfinished Literal Commentary on Genesis* Augustine thinks of the movement of the angels as the movement of their thought, as in this passage:

T6. . . . the question arises whether, apart from the movement of material bodies, there can be time in the movements of an immaterial creature such as the soul is, or the mind itself. This certainly experiences movement in its thoughts and in this movement there is something that comes first, and something that comes next, and this cannot be understood without some interval of time. If we accept this, then it can be readily understood that there was a time even before heaven and earth, if the angels were made before heaven and earth, because that means there was already a creature which would move time along by immaterial movements . . . (3.8)

Still, there is a problem for Augustine concerning the "days" referred to in the Genesis story of creation. According to that story, God did not create the heavenly bodies until the fourth day. Thus there were three days before the heavenly bodies appeared. Was not that time measured by days, even if those days were not broken down into hours? If so, then there was measured time before God created the heavenly bodies.

Augustine responds to this worry by refusing to allow that the first three days of creation, before God created the heavenly bodies, were really what we understand days to be. "What kind of days these are," he writes, "is difficult or even impossible for us to imagine, to say nothing of describing them" (City of God 11.6).

How much disorder, we may ask, does Augustine assign to the period of unmeasured time? Is it enough so that there would really have been no such thing as a first time, just time in general? It is hard to be certain about this. Augustine does say that, in this period, "not everything could be simultaneous." But he could have said that to make clear that a single thought of a given angel would have come after some other thought of that same angel and so would not be simultaneous with the other thought. Still, as in modern relativity theory, there would perhaps be no such thing as strict simultaneity among the thoughts of different angels. If so, then perhaps there would have been no such thing as the first moment of time.

Suppose, however, that Augustine did, as seems likely, accept the idea that there was a first angelic thought and so a first time. Given his assumption that motion is a precondition for time, he could not think there was a time when that angel existed motionless, that is, thoughtless. There is, however, another problem to be considered. Strictly speaking, no motion occurs at a point in time anyway. It is only during some period of time, no matter how short, that there can be motion. So how could there have been a first moment of time?

What Augustine could say is this:

(A3) There was some time t, such that, for any period of time after t, no matter how brief, some angel was in motion during that period; and for no period before t, no matter how brief, was anything in motion.

Assuming, with Augustine, that the idea of angelic motion is an acceptable one, (A3) seems to be an appropriate Augustinian interpretation of (A).

So far I have drawn on Books 11 and 12 to give an account of Augustine's views on time and creation. This part of the *City of God* was probably written around the year 417. Almost two decades earlier Augustine had written a quite different account of time in Book 11 of his *Confessions*. The earlier account is his most famous discussion of time. In fact, at least among philosophers today, that earlier account may be the most famous passage in the whole Augustinian corpus. That the earlier account is very different from the one we find in *The City of God* is suggested by this passage from the earlier one:

> T7. Let no one tell me then that time is the movements of heavenly bodies. At a man's prayer the sun stood still, so that a battle could be carried through to victory (*Joshua* 10.12ff): the sun stopped but time went on. (*Confessions* 11.13.30)

This passage does not say that when God made the sun stand still, nothing else moved. In fact, the very point of God's stopping the movement of the sun was to give Joshua and his army more time to carry the battle to victory. Still, Augustine does not add that the time they had in which to win the battle could only have been disordered time. One gets the impression from this and other passages in *Confessions* 11 that time is essentially something different from the measure of any particular body.

How could this be? Did Augustine simply change his mind about the nature of time? If he did, what made him change his mind? If he did not, how can *Confessions* 11 be reconciled with Books 11 and 12 of the *City of God*?

In *Confessions* 11 Augustine raises the Parmenidean question "Why then?" somewhat indirectly by reporting the skeptic's cheeky challenge 'What was God doing before He made heaven and earth?' (11.10.12). If we cannot think what might have occupied God's attention before the creation, the implication seems to be that we shall have to say God was simply idle, perhaps for an eternity, before He created the world. No doubt the skeptic who asks, "Why did God create the universe then?" would want to add the further, needling, question "What could there have possibly been about the particular moment that God chose for creation that made it different from all other moments?" After all, each moment without a world would seem to be, in itself, exactly like every other worldless moment in all relevant respects.

Augustine first responds to the skeptic's cheeky challenge with an abusive reply: "He was preparing hell for people who inquire into [such] profundities." But then he moves quickly to dismiss the question as ill-conceived. "Before God made heaven and earth," Augustine writes, "He was not doing anything" (11.12.14). Augustine's point is that by his act of creation he also created time itself. (See T1 above.) Up to this point the account in *Confessions* 11 coincides with the account in *City of God* 11 and 12.

But what would it be, on the view presented in *Confessions* 11, for God to create time? We cannot answer that question, Augustine indicates, unless we know what time is. We have already seen that, in his later discussion, he understands time to be the measure of motion. Here he proceeds rather differently. Moreover, he moves toward a different conclusion. In a justly famous expression of philosophical perplexity, quite the equal of anything we can find in Plato (who put many such expressions of perplexity in the mouth of his character, Socrates), Augustine writes:

T8. What then is time? Provided no one asks me, I know [what time is]. If I want to explain it to someone who asks me, I do not know. (11.14.17)

How does Augustine deal with this philosophical perplexity? He first reminds himself of an important truth about time. He reminds himself that we speak of long times and short times. Whatever time is, then, it is something that comes in long and short segments.

Augustine next focuses on present time, which he takes to be the only time that exists. After all, he reasons, the future is not yet and the past is no more. Only the present really exists.

Augustine asks himself whether present time can be long. Well, he notes, we do refer to "the present century," and a hundred years is certainly a long time. But, as Augustine goes on to point out, if, say, one year of the present century has passed, that part of the present century is no more. And if we have 98 years of the century yet to come, only one year is really present. But is even the present year really and truly present? Well, if so and so many months have already passed and so are no more, and so-and so many months are future and so are not yet; only that one month is really present.

Similar reasoning will, of course, apply to the present month, the present week, the present day, the present hour – even the present minute. In fact, for any *period* of time we call "present," no matter how short it may be, part of it will be already past and part will still be future. Only if we consider *now* to be a "knife-edge," an instant without any duration at all, can we find something that is truly present. But such a "knife-edge" instant cannot be long or short; it has no duration. And so, by our initial assumption about time, namely, that times are long or short, such an instant is not time. So, it seems, there is no such thing as time.

Eventually Augustine finds, as he supposes, a way out of this impasse. He focuses on a line from a hymn, 'God, creator of all things [*Deus creator omnium*].' Even to understand this line, we must hold the various syllables together in our mind. Thinking about what we are saying, as we say it, whether aloud or simply to ourselves, we can note that some of the syllables of this phrase are longer than others. And there are gaps between the words. Those observations lead Augustine to the thought that we measure time in our minds. We line up a sequence of sounds, or events, in our minds. We measure the parts of the sequence against each other and we measure the whole by reference to its parts. He refers to these as "my times," that is, my periods of time. Augustine writes:

> T9. So it is in you, my mind, that I measure my times. (11.27.37)

From T9 Augustine is led to conclude that time is a "distension," a spreading out. But a spreading out of what? Perhaps of the mind itself (11.26.33). His thought is that the only place where *periods* of time exist is in the mind. Thus

(α) Time is the measure of something mental.

This conclusion must be contrasted with the conclusions of *City of God* 11 and 12:

(β) Time is the measure of motion.
(γ) (Fully) ordered time is the measure of heavenly motion.

A good way to understand the difference between (α) and the conjunction of (β) and (γ) is to draw on a distinction we owe to the British philosopher J. M. E. McTaggart. McTaggart wrote an influential article early in the twentieth century in which he distinguished between what he called "A-series" terms, such as 'past,' 'present,' and 'future,' and "B-series" terms, such as 'precedes,' 'follows,' and 'is simultaneous with.'[2] The B-series terms enable us to place events on a time line, what is sometimes called the "fourth-dimension."

The A-series terms seem to pick out something that flows, or passes. Thus what is now future will become present and then move into the past. By contrast, if event e_1 comes before event e_2, that same relationship of temporal priority holds whether e_1 and e_2 belong to the future, the present, or the past.

A-series terms are essential for us agents to act in time. B-series terms are not enough. Thus if I have a meeting at 2 p.m. on October 12, I will know that the meeting begins after 1 p.m. and before 3 p.m. But I will not know whether I should put on my coat and prepare to go to the meeting unless I know what time it is *now*.

A-series terms, unlike terms in the B-series, function indexically. Their meaning is tied to the occasion of their use. Just as indexical terms such as 'this' and 'here' pick out different things on different occasions of their use, so do 'now,' 'in the future,' and 'in the past.' For these reasons, A-series terms are radically different from B-series terms. There have been various attempts to reduce A-series terms to B-series terms, but no such attempt has been successful. What we have to say is that neither series is reducible to the other.

If neither series can be reduced to the other, can we do without one of the two? Some philosophers have argued that we can and should. In particular, some philosophers have argued that the A-series is illusory rather than real. One of my own teachers, D. C. Williams, wrote a famous article, "The myth of passage,"[3] in which he argued that time is simply a fourth dimension, on a par with the familiar three dimensions of height, width, and depth. The idea that time passes and that an event that was future will become present and then past is a myth.

Williams was right, I think, in supposing that we need only the B-series for science, But even though A-series terms play no role in a scientific description of the world, the temporal perspective each of us has simply by being a conscious agent and actor in time seems to be, if anything, more significant to us and the way we lead our lives than the purely objective time line on which moments and periods of time are arranged by the relations of preceding, following, and being coincident with. For me, now, the past is settled, the future is at least to some extent open to determination by choices I will make. The present is the locus of my current experience and the pivot for my reflections and judgments about the past and my decisions about the future. To suppose that "the real me" is on an objective time line ordered simply by B-series terms is to denigrate what is most real to me.

Can the Augustine of *Confessions* 11 make a place for the objective time of the B-series without denying the lived time of the A-series? I think he can. He can understand the B-series time line as a human construction, something each of us can make for ourselves and coordinate with our society by using observations of the sun, clocks, and other time checks. But the "real" time, that is, human time, is something we put together mentally from, as Augustine puts it, anticipation, experience, and memory. He writes:

> T10. Who therefore can deny that the future does not yet exist? Yet already in the mind there is an expectation of the future. Who can deny that the past does not now exist. Yet there is still in the mind a memory of the past. None can deny that present time lacks any extension since it passes in a flash. Yet attention is continuous, and it is through this that what will be present progresses toward being absent. (11.28.37)

In chapter 1 I used Thomas Nagel's striking phrase 'the view from nowhere' to characterize the "objective," third-person view of reality.

Applied to time, an objectivist like my old teacher Donald Williams seeks a perspective from "nowhen," that is, a perspective from which there is no privileged "now," no privileged point on the time line.

Augustine, in *Confessions* 11 reverses the priority. Fundamental for him is an understanding of time from the perspective of "now." From this perspective, the objective time line is what we might call a "well-founded fiction," a fiction constructed in the mind of the individual thinker.

How are we to reconcile these two very different accounts of time? Did Augustine simply change his mind from the time he wrote *Confessions* 11 to the time he wrote *City of God* 11 and 12? That used to be my own view. I am now inclined to say that the two accounts complement each other.

Augustine seems to have written his *Unfinished Literal Commentary on Genesis* before he even started on his *Confessions*. There is no hint of the subjective theory of time in the earlier work. In the Books 11 and 12 of the *City of God*, written perhaps two or more decades after the unfinished work on Genesis, Augustine picked up and developed further his ideas about the angels and the beginning of time. Moreover, there is in the *City of God* no discussion of the subjective account of time. I am now inclined to think that Augustine's two different accounts of time reflect the contrast between the A-series and the B-series that McTaggart is famous for calling to our attention some 16 centuries later.

If this is the right way to think about Augustine's two different accounts of time, then we should add that, just as he offers us an account of A-series time that is distinct from his account of B-series time, so he also suggests two different ways in which God created time. According to Augustine, God created the measured time of the B-series by creating things that move and change. But He would have created A-series time by creating minds that experience the present, remember the past, and anticipate the future.

Augustine's idea that B-series time is the measure of motion has a clear antecedent in Aristotle. In Book 4 of his *Physics* Aristotle had claimed that "time is the number [or measure] of motion in respect of before and after" (220a24–5). Aristotle did also remark, almost in an aside, "But one might puzzle over whether if soul did not exist time would exist or not" (*Physics* 4.14, 223a21–2). However, unlike Augustine, he did nothing to develop a subjective account of time.

What we have to say, I think, is that Augustine's special contribution to the philosophy of time is to have called our philosophical attention to the lived time of the A-series. It is not what, according to Genesis 1:14, God created the heavens to measure. It is rather what you and I have in our minds, simply by virtue of being conscious and being actors in the world. It is time from our own individual, first-person perspective.

further reading

Richard Sorabji, *Time, Creation and the Continuum: Theories in Antiquity and in the Early Middle Ages*. London: Duckworth, 1983. One can hardly imagine a richer or more engrossing exploration of what the major and the minor figures of the ancient and early medieval period had to say about the questions discussed in this chapter.

notes

1 McKirahan translation, in R. D. McKirahan Jr., *Philosophy before Socrates* (Indianapolis: Hackett, 1994), p. 153.
2 "The unreality of time," *Mind* 17 (1908): 457–74.
3 *Journal of Philosophy* 48 (1951): 457–71.

faith and reason

With only slight exaggeration one could say that Augustine inaugurated the philosophical consideration of many topics that are now taken to be standard issues in the philosophy of religion. One of these is "Faith and Reason."

To be sure, several ancient Greek philosophers had interesting things to say about belief in the gods. Thus Xenophanes, who seems to have been born about 570 BCE, said some scathing things about the anthropomorphism of popular religion. "But if cattle and horses or lions had hands, or were able to draw with their hands and do the works that men can do," he is reported to have said, "horses would draw the forms of the gods like horses, and cattle like cattle, and they would make their bodies such as they each had themselves."[1] Xenophanes himself developed a monotheistic theology. But we have no evidence of anything he said about religious faith and how it is, or should be, related to reason and argumentation.

Plato had a great deal to say about gods, and about belief in gods. His dialogue *Euthyphro* is one of the most profound explorations in our philosophical tradition about whether morality[2] can be understood in any satisfactory way as doing what finds divine favor, as doing what "the gods love." The upshot seems to be that, if the gods have good reasons for approving of what they approve of and disapproving of what they disapprove of, we should look to those reasons to determine what we should do and not do. If they do not have good reasons, then divine favor is hardly a suitable basis for determining what we should do or refrain from doing.

Some people have read the *Euthyphro* as a critique of all religious belief and practice. But that reading goes well beyond anything explicit in the dialogue. One could say that the dialogue offers a critique of the claim that religious practice can have a rational justification. But it has nothing to say about religious faith in general, or about whether such faith can or should be supported or supplemented with philosophical arguments.

A tantalizing passage on that last question can be found in Plato's dialogue *The Sophist*:

> T1. Stranger: Must we not attribute the coming-into-being of these things out of nonbeing to divine craftsmanship and nothing else? Or are we to fall in with the belief that is commonly expressed?
> Theaetetus: What belief do you mean?
> Stranger: That nature gives birth to them as a result of some spontaneous cause that generates without intelligence. Or shall we say that they come from a cause which, working with reason and art, is divine and proceeds from divinity?
> Theaetetus: Perhaps because I am young, I often shift from one belief to the other, but at this moment, looking at your face and believing you to hold that these things have a divine origin, I too am convinced.
> Stranger: Well said, Theaetetus. If I thought you were the sort of person that might believe otherwise in the future, I should now try by force of persuasion to make you accept that account. But I can see clearly that, without any arguments of mine, your nature will come of itself to the conclusion which you tell me attracts you at this moment. So I will let it pass . . . (265cd)[3]

Plato does not let the Stranger explain how he might have tried, "by force of persuasion," to make Theaetetus accept his doctrine of divine creation. Presumably he would have used what has come to be called the "Argument from Design." Plato does present a divine creation story of his own in his dialogue *Timaeus*. But he does not argue that we can reason from the evidence of purpose in nature that some such story as the one he tells must be true. Nor does he explore further what the relationship is, or ought to be, between reasoning and belief in God.

Aristotle developed an argument for the Unmoved Mover, which St. Thomas Aquinas later used in his Five Ways for demonstrating *quia* (i.e., from effects to their cause) the existence of God. But Aristotle himself really had nothing to say about religious belief, and hence nothing about how such belief might, or might not, be supported or supplemented by philosophical arguments.

Tertullian (ca. 160–230 CE) is credited with having said, "I believe because it is absurd" (*credo quia absurdum est*). Although he seems not to have used those exact words, he did say things close enough to give him credit for marking out the position called "fideism," according to which only a doctrine that in some ways defies reason is a suitable candidate for religious faith.

It is, however, Augustine who first tries to make clear, from the position of a religious believer, what the role of reason should be in the life of a philosophically reflective believer. In many passages he speaks of "faith in search of understanding," a motto which St. Anselm, six and a half centuries later, first used as the title for what he finally decided to call the *Proslogion*, in which he presents his Ontological Argument for the existence of God.

In the dialogue *On Free Choice of the Will* Augustine asks his interlocutor, Evodius, whether he is certain that God exists (2.2.5.12). Evodius answers that he accepts this by faith, not by reason. Augustine then asks Evodius what he would say to a fool who had said in his heart, echoing a verse from the Psalms, "There is no God."

Evodius responds to Augustine's challenge by suggesting an appeal to the evidence of the biblical scriptures. But Augustine is not satisfied with that response. Why then, he asks, should we not simply accept the authority of the scriptural writers on other matters, rather than engage in our own philosophical investigation? Evodius replies, "We want to know and understand (*nosse et intellegere*) what we believe" (2.2.5.16).

Augustine compliments Evodius on his having grasped the nature of their joint project, which is to come to understand what they hold by faith. Appealing to the "Old Latin" text of Isaiah 7:9, *Nisi credideritis, non intellegetis* ("Unless you have believed, you will not understand," as well as to the admonition of Jesus "Seek and you shall find" – John 17: 3), Augustine reaffirms that their purpose is to try to understand what they believe. (Incidentally, modern translations, based on a better Hebrew text, read the sentence this way: "If you will not believe, surely you shall not be established," which altogether fails to make Augustine's point.)

An obvious question to ask is whether one might gain faith through developing one's understanding, as well as gain understanding by developing one's faith. Augustine, in one of his sermons (43.3.4), acknowledges, what is any case obvious, that his hearers cannot believe of what he is saying that it is true unless they understand his words. But it is one of the central claims of his philosophical theology that, at least in matters of religious or spiritual significance, faith must precede understanding. Thus in his *Tractate* 29 on the Gospel of John, he writes, "If you have not understood, I say, 'Believe!' For understanding is the reward of faith." He adds, "Therefore do not seek to understand that you may believe, but believe that you may understand." (*Ergo noli quaerere intelligere ut credas, sed crede ut intelligas.*)

Let us return now to Book 2 of *On Free Choice of the Will*. After listing two additional items in the search they are about to undertake, Augustine suggests they begin their inquiry with the question 'Do you yourself exist?' He continues with this passage I quoted in chapter 1:

T2. Are you perhaps afraid that you might be deceived by this questioning? But if you did not exist, you could in no way be deceived. (2.3.7.20)

The reader might be led by this move to expect that Augustine would try to develop a proof of God's existence based on the foundational certainty of one's own existence. But he does not do that. Instead Augustine gets Evodius to agree that it would not be clear to him that he existed unless he were alive and also understood that he is alive. That move leads Augustine to introduce a scale of being, with inanimate things at the bottom of the scale, living beings higher up, and, among living beings, those with understanding higher than those that, even though they have perception, lack understanding.

Although it may not be immediately obvious to the reader, Augustine's aim in introducing the idea of a scale of being is to be able to specify God as a being who is so high up on such a scale that there is nothing higher. At the bottom of the scale Augustine places a stone, which is his example of an inanimate being. Above such inanimate things he places beasts, which are living things that lack understanding. Above the beasts he places human beings, who are both alive and have understanding (2.3.7.22–3).

A little later on, at 2.6.13.52, Augustine develops a parallel hierarchy of natures, or souls. In this parallel hierarchy he places on the bottom rung (i) the nature of a stone, (ii) the soul of a beast on the next level, and, finally, (iii) the rational soul or mind of a human being on the third level. Augustine asks Evodius whether, if they found something superior to our reason, he would agree that the entity they had found was God. Evodius says that being better (*melius*) than the best thing in him would be, just by itself, insufficient to guarantee that this being was God; to be God, he says, an entity would have to be something to whom nothing is superior (*quo est nullus superior*, 2.6.14.54). This comment suggests the following definition of 'God':

(D) x is God = df x is superior to the human mind (or rational soul) and nothing is superior to x.

With this definition in mind, Augustine, in his *On Free Choice of the Will*, begins a long discussion of truth that culminates in the conclusion that truth is superior to our minds:

T3. And so it is clear beyond any doubt that this one truth, by which people become wise, and which makes them judges, not of it, but of other things, is better than our minds.

Now you had conceded that if I proved the existence of something higher than our minds, you would admit that it was God, as long as there was nothing higher still. I accepted this concession, and said that it would be enough if I proved that there is something higher than our minds. For if there is something more excellent than the truth, then that is God; if not, the truth itself is God. So in either case you cannot deny that God exists . . . (2.14.38.152–15.39.153)[4]

Regimenting the argument in T2 somewhat, we could put it in this form:

(1) Anything that is more excellent than our minds and to which nothing is superior is God. [from Definition (D) above]
(2) Truth is more excellent than our minds.
    Therefore,
(3) Either truth is God or something superior to truth is God.
    Therefore,
(4) God exists.[5]

This argument for the existence of God is the first in a long line of such proofs offered by Christian and Muslim philosophers throughout the Middle Ages into the seventeenth century. Augustine's argument is, no doubt, one of the least impressive of these arguments, but it is a start. When Anselm produced what has come to be called the "ontological argument" in his *Proslogion*, near the end of the eleventh century, he began the crucial chapter 2 with these very Augustinian-sounding words: "Then, Lord, you who give understanding to faith, give me to understand, as much as you see fit, that you exist, just as we believe [you do], and that you are what we believe [you to be]." Anselm goes on, of course, to produce a line of reasoning that has been one of the most discussed arguments in the whole history of Western philosophy. Augustine's argument, by contrast, rates little more than a 'Good try!' But it does mark the beginning of a project that continues right up to the present time.

What Augustine has to say about the other main topics of *On Free Choice of the Will* is much more impressive than his argument for the existence of God. His treatment of the Problem of Divine Foreknowledge and Human Free Will, which we shall take up in the next chapter, frames that problem in a way that makes it urgent for all later philosophy of religion. Moreover, Augustine's suggestions about how to resolve the problem are still worth considering.

The other chief problem Augustine takes up in *On Free Choice of the Will* is the Problem of Evil, which we shall discuss in chapter 12. Again, Augustine's formulation of the problem is canonical and his attempted solutions are among the live options to be considered even today.

What does Augustine think he is doing when he tries to solve the Problem of Divine Foreknowledge, or the Problem of Evil? Both of these problems are skeptical challenges to religious belief. They both pose issues that seem to stand in the way of orthodox Christian belief. If

Augustine can solve, or resolve, or somehow disarm these problems he will thereby have removed an obstacle to faith. So in these cases, 'faith in search of understanding' seems to mean (1) *faith in search of rational ways to remove the obstacles to faith.*

A special case of (1) would be Augustine's attempt in his treatise *On the Trinity* to make intelligible the doctrine that God is three-in-one. Many people find the Doctrine of the Trinity to be incoherent. Augustine's task in his treatise is to render the doctrine coherent. After announcing his goal for the rest of the work in the preface to Book 8, Augustine writes, "Meanwhile let us hold fast to this rule, that what has not yet become clear to our intellect may still be preserved by the firmness of our faith."

The effort to produce an argument for the existence of God seems to be something rather different. It is not produced in response to an identifiable problem in the claim that God exists. So why do we need a proof that God exists, if we already have a firm belief that God exists?

Augustine's answer seems to be given in this passage, again from Book 2 of *Free Choice of the Will*:

T4. Then, to those who believed, [Jesus Christ] said, "Seek and ye shall find." For what is believed without being known cannot be said to have been found, and no one can become fit for finding God unless he believes first what he shall know afterwards. (2.2.6.18)

What Augustine seems to be saying here is that faith in God appropriately seeks knowledge of God. Believers in God have often supposed that they could gain knowledge of God through religious experience. In his writings Augustine describes several mystical visions. Two descriptions are to be found in his *Confessions*, one in Book 7 (at 7.10.16) and one in Book 9 (at 10.24–5).

Augustine, however, seems to think that philosophical reflection can help us to know God. And so faith in search of understanding can include faith in search of philosophical reflections on what must be the nature of God. And so we have a second meaning for 'faith in search of understanding': (2) *faith in God in search of an understanding of what God's nature must be.* Thus in the latter half of his treatise *On the Trinity* Augustine uses the analogy of the human mind, to understand the Divine Trinity.

There is yet a third meaning for 'faith in search of understanding' that informs Augustine's writing. Augustine supposes that the Holy Scriptures are the revealed word of God. In a way he is what would be called today a "biblical fundamentalist." But in a more important way he is not a biblical fundamentalist at all. Although he firmly believes that what the Bible says is true, he allows himself tremendous latitude in interpreting scriptural passages. Sometimes he comes up with a number of alternative interpretations of a given verse of scripture. Here, in a crucial passage from Book 12 of his *Confessions* he draws the distinction between truth and meaning as a distinction between, for example, the truth of the creation story in the book of Genesis and the intention of the human writer, whom he takes to be Moses:

> T5. I see that two areas of disagreement can arise, when something is recorded by truthful reporters using signs. The first concerns the truth of the matter in question. The second concerns the intention of the writer. It is one thing to inquire into the truth about the origin of the creation. It is another to ask what understanding of the words on the part of a reader and hearer was intended by Moses, a distinguished servant of your faith. (12.23.32)

Augustine has just been puzzling over the meaning of the first verse of the first chapter of Genesis. He has come up with five different interpretations:

> T6. On the basis of all these axioms, a view may be urged to this effect: "In the beginning God made heaven and earth" means that by his Word coeternal with himself, God made the intelligible and sensible (or spiritual and corporeal) worlds. Another view could be that "In the beginning God made heaven and earth" means that by his Word coeternal with himself, God made the universal mass of this physical world with all the natures it contains, manifest and well known to us. A third view might be that "In the beginning God made heaven and earth" means that by his Word coeternal with himself he made the formless matter of the spiritual and physical creation. A fourth view might be that "God made heaven and earth" means that by his Word coeternal with himself God made the formless matter of the physical creation, when heaven and earth were still chaotic, though we now perceive them to be distinct and endowed with forms in the physical world. A fifth view might say, "In the beginning God made heaven and earth' means at the very start of his making and working, God made formless matter containing in a confused condition heaven and earth, but now they are given form and are manifest to us, with all the things that are in them. (12.20.29)

It might be hard for an ordinary reader to imagine what distinctions Augustine has in mind when he offers these five possibilities. But it is safe to say that Augustine spent an important part of his life thinking about such matters. Many of the considerations he adduces in favor of one interpretation over another are aimed at making this verse of Scripture as understandable as possible, not only in itself, but also in the context of the whole creation story.

So here is an example of Augustine's faith in search of understanding that is not either an effort to remove obstacles to faith nor an effort to achieve knowledge that what one believes is true but rather this: (3) *faith in search of understanding what it is that one believes.*

This third understanding of 'faith in search of understanding' is paradoxical. Surely we know what we believe, do we not, even if we do not know whether what we believe is true?

In fact there are many important questions about what I believe that I cannot answer immediately. Do I believe that affirmative action is sometimes, never, or always, a good policy in college admissions? I may have to reflect a long time about this question before I can say what I believe.

Of course, Augustine's questions about what one believes, who believes that God made heaven and earth, are very different from the question about what one believes, who believes in having an affirmative action policy. In the creation issue I am, if I accept the first verse of Genesis as my own belief, accepting as true what some biblical writer (presumably not Moses!) wrote. But, as Augustine points out in the discussion surrounding T5, we are no longer able to question the original author of that statement about what it means. We have to make sense of it for ourselves in the light of whatever textual, theological, and philosophical considerations we can bring to bear on the issue.

Christian faith, like Jewish and Muslim faith, rests in important part on what are taken to be sacred scriptures. Any believer in one of these traditions needs to develop an understanding of the meaning of those scriptures. That is the third meaning that Augustine assigns to his motto 'Faith in search of understanding.'

One might well want to reflect on why anyone, including Augustine, should deem it fitting to assign special status to writings taken to be sacred scriptures. Indeed, one might want to reflect on what it means to call certain writings "sacred." But one should not assume that, just because Augustine came to believe that certain writings are sacred, he took those writings to be immune to fresh assessment in the light of scientific discoveries. That is hardly the case. Augustine seems open to an appeal to scientific findings to narrow down what might be the correct interpretation of a passage in Scripture. In fact, Galileo could plausibly take Augustine to be his ally in his effort to win ecclesiastical support for his own scientific findings.

Among the Augustinian texts that Galileo quoted to make a case for the acceptability of his own scientific findings is this passage from Book 1 of *The Literal Meaning of Genesis*:

T7. Whenever the experts of this world can truly demonstrate something about natural phenomena, we should show it not to be contrary to our Scripture; but whenever in their books they teach something contrary to the Holy Writ, we should without any doubt hold it to be false and also show this by any means we can; and in this way we should keep the faith of our Lord, in whom are hidden all the treasures of knowledge, in order not to be seduced by the verbosity of false philosophy or frightened by the superstition of fake religion.[6]

Galileo interprets T7 this way:

T8. These words imply, I think, the following doctrine: in the learned books of worldly authors are contained some propositions about nature which are truly demonstrated and others which are simply taught; in regard to the former, the task of wise theologians is to show that they are not contrary to Holy Scripture; as for the latter (which are taught but not demonstrated with necessity), if they contain anything contrary to the Holy Writ, they must be considered indubitably false and must be demonstrated such by every possible means. So physical conclusions which have been truly demonstrated should not be given a lower place than scriptural passages, but rather one should clarify how such passages do not contradict those conclusions . . .[7]

As we have already seen, Augustine allows himself considerable latitude in interpreting Holy Scripture. It is, I think, quite reasonable to suppose that Augustine would not have seen the rise of modern science to which Galileo contributed so significantly as a threat to his Christian faith, or to the status he accorded the Christian Bible.

further reading

John M. Rist, *Augustine: Ancient Thought Baptized*. Cambridge: Cambridge University Press, 1994, ch. 3 ("Certainty, belief and understanding"). This chapter of Rist's book is a provocative and wide-ranging discussion of some of the issues raised here.

notes

1 G. S. Kirk, J. E. Raven, and M. Schofield, *The Presocratic Philosophers*, 2nd edition (Cambridge: Cambridge University Press, 1983), p. 169.

2 Actually, piety (*to hosion*), but his line of questioning is easily generalized and made into a discussion of the defensibility of what is called the "Divine Command Theory" of morality.

3 F. M. Cornford (tr.), *The Republic of Plato* (London: Oxford University Press, 1941).

4 *On Free Choice of the Will*, tr. Thomas Williams (Indianapolis: Hackett, 1993), p. 58.

5 This argument is, of course, open to many objections. For example, Augustine has not ruled out the possibility of there being two or more entities, each superior to truth, but each such that nothing is superior to it. Nor has he here tried to make plausible the idea that God might simply be truth.

6 This is an English translation of Galileo's rendering of a section of *The Literal Interpretation of Genesis* 1.21.41, taken from Maurice A. Finocchiaro, *The Galileo Affair: A Documentary History* (Berkeley: University of California Press, 1989), p. 101.

7 Ibid., pp. 101–2.

foreknowledge and free will

Early in Book 3 of Augustine's dialogue *On Free Choice of the Will* Augustine's discussion partner, Evodius, makes a sensible, but potentially troubling, point. Unless, he says, the movement of one's will toward its object were voluntary and within one's power, one would not be praiseworthy when one turns to the higher objects, or blameworthy when one turns to lower objects instead (3.1.3.13). Evodius then adds this stunning question: 'How can it be, if God foreknows everything that will happen in the future, that we do not sin by necessity?' (3.2.4.14).

Augustine immediately recognizes the perplexity that troubles Evodius and tries to develop it further. Applying his expansion to the sample case of Adam, we get this philosophical conundrum:

(1) If God foreknows that Adam will sin, then it is necessary that Adam sin.
(2) If it is necessary that Adam sin, Adam does not sin of his own free will.
(3) If Adam does not sin of his own free will, then he is not blameworthy for his sin.
But: (4) Adam is blameworthy for his sin. (3.3.6.21)

This is a classic skeptical argument in the philosophy of religion. It seems to force us to either give up the claim that God, being omniscient, foreknows that Adam will sin, or else give up the assumption that Adam is blameworthy. This conundrum is still discussed today. Moreover, it is Augustine's formulation of the argument early in Book 3 of his *On Free Choice of the Will* that has framed the issue for the succeeding 16 centuries.

The problem of foreknowledge and free will is, in fact, not entirely original with Augustine. He himself, in Book 5 of his *City of God*, credits

Cicero with calling the problem to his attention. But Cicero was a theological skeptic. For him, the problem was a good argument for concluding that if human beings are culpable for their misdeeds, it is not the case that there is a God with foreknowledge of those deeds. Augustine writes:

> T1. [Cicero] constrains the soul to this dilemma, forcing it to choose between those propositions: either there is some scope for our will, or there is foreknowledge. He thinks that both cannot be true; to affirm one is to deny the other. If we choose foreknowledge, free will is annihilated; if we choose free will, foreknowledge is abolished. And so, being a man of eminent learning, a counselor of wide experience and practiced skill in matters of human life, Cicero chooses free will. (*City of God* 5.9)

Although Augustine is a great admirer of Cicero, his own situation is quite different from Cicero's. By the time he came to write Book 3 of *On Free Choice of the Will*, he had been baptized as a Christian, ordained as a priest, and was about to become the Bishop of Hippo. So whereas Cicero could happily use the argument above to prove that there is no God who foreknows that Adam will sin, Augustine's commitments lead him to try to disable one or more of the premises.

Many solutions have been proposed to the problem of foreknowledge and free will. Some of the most interesting can be found, either explicitly stated, or at least suggested, by Augustine himself in *On Free Choice of the Will*. Here is the first solution Augustine proposes:

the guarantor solution

> T2. *Our will would not be a will, unless it were in our power. Therefore, because it is in our power, it is free . . . Nor can it be a will if it is not in our power, Therefore, God also has foreknowledge of our power. So the power is not taken from me by His foreknowledge, but because of His foreknowledge, the power to will will more certainly be present in me . . .*
>
> (3.3.8.33–5)

This is the solution that Augustine seems most satisfied with. Thus, in Book 5 of his *City of God*, written decades after *On Free Choice of the Will*, this is the solution Augustine returns to. He states it there in this way:

> T3. It does not follow, then, that there is nothing in our will because God foreknew what was going to be in our will; for if he foreknew this, it was not nothing that he foreknew. Further, if, in foreknowing what would be in our will, he foreknew something, and not nonentity, it follows immediately that there is something in our will, even if God foreknows it. Hence

we are in no way compelled either to preserve God's foreknowledge by abolishing our free will, or to safeguard our free will by denying (blasphemously) the divine foreknowledge. (*City of God* 5.10)

The Guarantor Solution allows God to have, not just foreknowledge of what Adam will do, but also foreknowledge of what he will do *of his own free will*:

(1*) If God foreknows that Adam will sin of his own free will, then it is necessary that Adam sin of his own free will.

But now, instead of (2), we will want this:

(2*) If it is necessary that Adam sin of his own free will, then Adam sins of his own free will.

Instead of God's foreknowledge being a threat to Adam's free will, it can actually *guarantee* Adam's free will. What are we to make of this move?

It seems that Augustine, by having God foreknow what Adam will do of his own free will, has removed the threat foreknowledge poses for free will. But there are still things to worry about. Suppose:

(2a*) It is necessary that Adam sin of his own free will.

Still, this will be true:

(2a) It is necessary that Adam sin.

Is it conceivable that Adam sin of his own free will, even though Adam could not have failed to sin? Many, perhaps most, philosophers have found this inconceivable. They have assumed what Harry Frankfurt calls "the principle of alternative possibilities" (PAP). According to PAP, one is not morally responsible for an action unless one could have done otherwise, that is, unless one could have performed some alternative action or simply chosen not to act.[1] Given that Augustine supposes one is not morally praiseworthy or blameworthy, and hence not morally responsible for an action, unless one acted of one's own free will, accepting PAP means that one does not act of one's own free will unless one could have done otherwise.

Frankfurt has argued, persuasively, I think, that PAP is false. His defense of his rejection of that principle includes a number of thought experiments. Here is a very simple thought experiment, one of my own devising, that calls PAP into question.

Suppose I am voting, using a voting machine, for the president of the student government. Suppose that this particular machine is rigged to register every vote as a vote for Barbara Smith. And suppose that I, being a supporter of Barbara's, click on the icon for Barbara Smith. Suppose I do this without any outside pressure, let alone compulsion, and in complete ignorance that, even if I had clicked on the icon for Barbara's competitor, my vote would have been counted as a vote for Barbara. I vote for Barbara Smith, am morally responsible for doing so and hence, according to Augustine, do so of my own free will, even though, given the rigged machine, I could not have done otherwise.[2]

Some philosophers today see in Frankfurt's rejection of PAP a way of reconciling moral responsibility with causal determinism. No less interesting, in my view, is the opportunity it presents to fill out Augustine's Guarantor Solution to the problem of foreknowledge and free will. God's foreknowledge that one will act freely will guarantee one's freedom in that action, even though God's foreknowledge of what one freely chooses to do will also guarantee the outcome of one's choice.

the divine-case solution

A second possibility for trying to show that God's foreknowledge need be no threat to free will is mentioned ever so fleetingly in *On Free Choice of the Will*. In the dialogue Augustine suggests to Evodius that God must have foreknowledge of his own actions. Evodius immediately agrees:

T4. Certainly if I say that God has foreknowledge of my deeds, I should say with even greater confidence that he has foreknowledge of his own acts, and foresees with complete certainty what he will do. (3.3.6.23)

Augustine then points out that by reasoning which parallels the case of Adam, we should say that God does not act of his own free will. But surely that conclusion is unacceptable.

The Divine-Case Solution does not help us pinpoint what is wrong with the original argument. In particular, it does not help us determine which premise to reject, let alone, why we should reject it. But it does suggest that something must be wrong. To suppose that God does not have foreknowledge of His own actions is to reject His omniscience. But to conclude that He does not act of His own free will is to limit His autonomy. Something must be wrong.

Disappointingly, Augustine does not pursue this solution any further. In the dialogue Evodius retracts his claim that God foreknows his own actions. "When I said that everything that God foreknows," he says, "I considered only those things that happen in His creation, not, however, what happens in Himself; since things don't happen in Him; they are eternal." In this way we move directly from the Divine-Case Solution to the Eternality Solution.

the eternality solution

Neither Evodius nor Augustine develops the idea of God's eternal present here in *On Free Choice of the Will*. But Augustine develops it elsewhere, especially in this eloquent passage from Book 11 of *The City of God*:

> T5. It is not with God as it is with us. He does not look ahead to the future, look directly at the present, look back at the past. He sees in some other manner, utterly remote from anything we experience or could imagine. He does not see things by turning his attention from one thing to another. He sees all without any kind of change. Things which happen under the condition of time are in the future, not yet in being, or in the present, already existing, or in the past, no longer in being. But God comprehends all these in a stable and eternal present. (11.21)

The idea of *fore*knowledge presupposes the ideas of past, present, and future, what, as we noted in Chapter 9, J. M. E. McTaggart called the "A-series," rather than a time dimension made up of instants and periods of time related to each by the relations of *before* and *after*. The latter, what McTaggart called the "B-series," is what, according to T5, God sees in His "eternal present." Thus, according to this view, there is, strictly speaking, no such thing as God's foreknowledge, that is, God's seeing into the future. For God everything that has happened, is happening, and will happen, is present.

Clever as the Eternality Solution is, there seems to be a way to translate what is worrying about God's foreknowledge into B-series talk. Conceiving foreknowledge in the usual A-series way (with past, present, and future) invites us to think of what has happened in the past as something settled, fully determined. One cannot change the past. So if I knew yesterday that you are going to the beach tomorrow, there is a kind of settledness about your going to the beach that derives from my foreknowledge. If I foreknew yesterday what you would be doing tomorrow, then what you will do tomorrow was already settled yesterday. That "settledness" robs you of the possibility of doing otherwise and so, it may seem, robs you of any free choice in the matter. Such "settledness" is something that, traditionally, has been called the "necessity of the past."

But wait! Would there not be the same settledness, or at least as much settledness, about my knowing at some time, T-1, that you will go to the beach at some later time, T-2, even if we do not think of either time as past or future? It seems so. If that is right, then perhaps the eternal present would be just as threatening to free will as foreknowledge is.

In fact, eternal presenthood does present its own threat to free will. We naturally think of the future as being open in a way that the past is not. This "openness," we think, provides room for alternative possibilities. However, if the future is laid out in God's eternal present in the same way that the past is, then what seems to us to be the openness of the future will be simply a product of our ignorance. In fact, the future will be just as settled as the past. So perhaps it is just as well that Augustine does not pursue the Eternality Solution to the problem of foreknowledge and free will.

That brings us to another attempt to solve the problem of foreknowledge and free will.

the modal-placement solution

The Modal-Placement Solution requires us to think about what exactly we are supposing to be necessary in Adam's sinning. Is it Adam's sinning, just by itself? Or is it the connection between God's foreknowledge and Adam's sinning?

To clarify things a bit it might be well to consider a different sort of example. It seems to be a necessary truth about horse racing that whatever horse, if any, crosses the finish line first wins the race. Thus:

(a) Necessarily, if Charger crosses the finish line first, then Charger wins.

Suppose now that Charger does in fact cross the finish line ahead of all the other horses.

(b) Charger crosses the finish line first.

Does that make it necessary that Charger win, so that Charger just had to win?

(c) Charger necessarily wins.

No. To infer (c) from (a) and (b) is to commit a modal fallacy. All (a) tells us is that there is a necessary connection between Charger's crossing the finish line first (if that is in fact what happens), and Charger's winning. It does not, even in conjunction with (b), give us an adequate reason for concluding that Charger had to win this race. All we may validly conclude from (a) and (b) is this:

(d) Charger wins.

In ordinary English, as in ordinary Latin, speakers tend to be rather sloppy about their placement of the "necessity operator." To make use of the Modal-Placement Solution to the problem of foreknowledge and free will we will need to be especially careful about what it is that is being said to be necessary. Thus we will make a clear distinction between these statements:

(5) Necessarily, if God foreknows that Adam will sin, then Adam will sin.
(6) If God foreknows that Adam will sin, then Adam will necessarily sin.

Later medieval philosophers characterized the difference between (5) and (6) as the difference between the *necessity of the conditional* and the *necessity of the consequent*.

Thus from (5) and

(7) God foreknows that Adam will sin.

This follows:

(8) Adam will sin.

But this does not follow from (5):

(9) Adam will necessarily sin.

To get (9) from (7) we need (6), the necessity of the consequent. The necessity of the conditional is not enough.

Boethius (480–524) seems to have been the first philosopher to mark this modal distinction clearly. But Augustine seems to be struggling to get at the point. Thus in *On Free Choice of the Will* he asks Evodius whether, if he foreknew that someone was going to sin, it would be necessary that he sin. Evodius answers that it would indeed be necessary (3.4.9.38). Evodius seems to be confusing the necessity of the conditional with the necessity of the consequent and thus supposing that every thing foreknown is something that is in itself necessary.

Augustine's reply "You do not compel someone to sin whom you foreknow will sin, although without doubt, he will sin" (3.4.9.39) might suggest to a reader the distinction between the necessity of the conditional and the necessity of the consequent. But Augustine does not himself offer this analysis.

By contrast, St. Anselm, writing almost seven centuries later, makes completely clear that he understands the Boethian distinction and is able to put it to effective use. He writes with characteristic succinctness in *De concordia* 1.3:

> T6. Therefore, when we say that what God foreknows is going to happen is necessarily going to happen, we are not asserting always that it is going to happen by necessity but simply that it is necessary that what is going to happen is going to happen.[3]

foreknowledge does not compel

Whether or not Augustine sees the point that the necessity of the conditional does not necessitate the consequent and so, for example, compel Adam to sin, he certainly makes the point that foreknowledge itself does not compel Adam to do what God foreknows he will do:

> T7. Unless I am mistaken, you would not directly compel the man to sin, though you knew beforehand that he was going to sin. Nor does your foreknowledge in itself compel him to sin even though he was certainly going to sin, as we must assume if you have real foreknowledge. (3.4.10.39)

In the next section of Book 3 Augustine backs up the claim in T7 with the analogy of memory, in this passage:

> T8. Just as you apply no compulsion to past events by having them in your memory, so God by his foreknowledge does not compel them to take place. As you remember certain things that you have done and yet have not done all the things that you remember, so God foreknows all the things of which He is the cause, and yet he is not the cause of all that he foreknows. (3.4.10.40)

Part of Augustine's idea here is that, with veridical memory, at any rate, we remember that something happened because it happened. It did not happen because we remember it. That is, our now remembering it is not the cause of its having happened. Going now in the other temporal direction, if we truly foreknow that something will happen, we truly foreknow it because, indeed, it will happen. But our foreknowledge is not the cause of its happening. And so it is, Augustine says, with God's foreknowledge.

Augustine had completed Book 3 of *On Free Choice of the Will* by 395. He had not completed Book 5 of the *City of God* until two decades later, in 415. The earlier work strikes us readers as more exploratory than the later one. Augustine is trying out various solutions to the problem he is addressing in the hope that at least one will be satisfactory.

The discussion in the later work is much less probing and much more settled than the one in *On Free Choice of the Will*. What he gives us in the *City of God* is simply the Guarantor Solution.

> T9. Thus our wills have only as much power as God has willed and foreknown; God, whose foreknowledge is infallible, has foreknown the strength of our wills and their achievements, and it is for that reason that their future strength is completely determined and their future achievements utterly assured. (5.9)

Among the achievements of our wills are, he supposes, many free actions. Their being the outcome of *free* choice, he thinks, is as fully guaranteed by God's foreknowledge as is the choice itself.

further reading

Linda T. Zagzebski, *The Dilemma of Freedom and Foreknowledge*. New York: Oxford University Press, 1991. This is a masterful survey of solutions to the problem.

notes

1 See Harry Frankfurt, "Alternative possibilities and moral responsibility," in *The Importance of What We Care About* (Cambridge: Cambridge University Press, 1988), pp. 1–10, for the original statement of Frankfurt's position. Frankfurt's piece has spawned a mountain of literature, pro and con, including ever more refined thought experiments.
2 Readers who have misgivings about my simple thought experiment, or who are simply interested in pursuing the topic further, are invited to explore the rather considerable literature Harry Frankfurt's rejection of PAP has inspired.
3 *De concordia*, tr. T. Birmingham, in B. Davies and G. R. Evans (eds.), *Anselm of Canterbury, the Major Works* (Oxford: Oxford University Press, 1998), pp. 435–74.

the problem of evil

We speak of *the* problem of evil, but, in fact, there are several distinct problems that are quite appropriately called "the problem of evil." Take, for example, the problem that the biblical book of Job presents. In the first verse of the first chapter of that book we are told that Job is "blameless and upright." A few verses later God Himself says of Job, "there is none like him on the earth, a blameless and upright man, who fears God and turns away from evil" (1:8). Yet as a test of the faithfulness of this blameless and upright man his herds are destroyed, his children are killed, and eventually he himself is afflicted with sores "from the sole of his foot to the crown of his head" (2:7).

The book of Job raises in some of the most eloquent writing in Western literature this wrenching question: 'Why do good people suffer and bad people prosper?' That problem of Divine justice has been taken to call for a theodicy, that is, an explanation of how it can be that God is just. And the problem it presents for a religious believer is one problem of evil.

David Hume attributes to the Hellenistic philosopher Epicurus a very different problem of evil. Here is the way Hume puts the problem:

> T1. Epicurus' old questions are yet unanswered.
>
> Is [God] willing to prevent evil, but not able? Then he is impotent. Is he able, but not willing? Then he is malevolent. Is he both able and willing? Whence then is evil?[1]

Hume thinks we face this trilemma: Either God is not all-powerful, or else He is not all-good, or else there is no evil. We can sharpen the force of the trilemma by putting the problem this way. The following three statements, it has seemed to many people, are inconsistent:

(1) God is omnipotent.
(2) God is omnibenevolent.
(3) There is evil.

We can give up (1) and allow that there are some things God cannot do, for example, eliminate all evil. Alternatively, we can hold onto the idea that God is all-powerful, but allow that God is not completely benevolent. Or else, and this is, according to Hume, the final alternative, we can hold firmly to God's omnipotence and omnibenevolence and deny the real existence of evil.

There are, course other options. To avoid inconsistency we could deny two, or even all three of these statements. In fact, we could of course simply deny that God exists. But, according to Hume, what we cannot do is consistently assert all three statements. They form what has been called an "inconsistent triad."

This Consistency Problem of Evil is very different from the Problem of Divine Justice posed by the Book of Job. That book never makes an issue of the mere existence of evil. The mere existence of evil is taken for granted. The problem posed in Job concerns the just distribution of rewards and punishments, or at least the just distribution of prosperity and suffering.

The Consistency Problem of Evil does not arise unless we assign "omni" attributes to God, in particular, the attribute of being able to do whatever He wants, plus the attribute of being all-good. The problem is then to understand how any evil at all could creep into a world controlled by a being that is all-powerful and, at the same time, completely good.

As I mentioned, Hume credits Epicurus with having raised the Consistency Problem of Evil. Perhaps Hume made this attribution on the basis of his reading of Cicero's *On the Nature of the Gods*, which is a discussion of Epicurean and Stoic theology.

It is not clear who first stated the Consistency Problem of Evil. Plato edges up to this problem in Book 2 of his *Republic*, where Socrates is made to say this:

> T2. Therefore, since a god is good, he is not, as most people claim, the cause of everything that happens to human beings but of only a few things, for good things are fewer than bad ones in our lives. He alone is responsible for the good things, but we must find some other cause for the bad ones, not a god. (379c)

We have in T2 the idea of pure goodness in God, and the idea that that, since there is evil, it must have another cause. One might infer that God is, therefore not all-powerful, or else God would have eliminated the cause of evil. But this solution to the Consistency Problem of Evil seems inconsistent with Socrates's teaching at the end of Book 6 of the *Republic*, where Socrates says this:

> T3. Therefore, you should also say that not only do the objects of knowledge owe their being known to the good, but their being is also due to it. (509b)

This passage seems to claim that everything there is, or at least everything there is that can be known, is caused by the good.

In any case, the solution suggested in T2 is not anything that Augustine can accept, since he supposes that God is all-powerful and hence able to prevent any other cause from bringing evil into the world.

Augustine was preoccupied with this problem of evil throughout much of his adult life. After being converted to philosophy by reading Cicero, Augustine tried to read the Christian Bible. He found it "unworthy" in comparison to Cicero.[2] Partly because of his perplexity over the origin of evil, he fell into the company of the Manicheans, a Christian, or semi-Christian, sect whose members believed that there is a principle of darkness, or evil, as well as a principle of light, or good. The Manicheans solved the Consistency Problem of Evil by denying that God is omnipotent.

Augustine became a Manichean hearer, or learner, and remained one for nine years. When he later became a Christian, in fact, a leading theologian of the Christian Church, he defined Manicheanism as a Christian heresy. But before Augustine could become a Christian, he needed to have a response to the Consistency Problem of Evil. In Book 7 of his *Confessions*, Augustine states the problem this way:

T4. Here is God and see what God has created. God is good and is most mightily and incomparably superior to these things. But, being God, he created good creatures. See how God surrounds and fills them. Then where and whence is evil? How did it creep in? What is its root and what is its seed? Or does it not have any being? Why should we fear and avoid what has no being? If our fear is vain, it is certain that fear itself is evil, and that the heart is groundlessly disturbed and tortured. And this evil is the worse for the fact that it has no being to be afraid of. Yet we still fear. Thus it is either evil that we fear or our fear which is evil. Where then does it come from, since the good God made everything good? Certainly the greatest and supreme Good made lesser goods; yet the Creator and all he created are good. What then is the origin of evil? Is it that the matter from which he made things was somehow evil? He gave it form and order, but did he leave in it an element which he could not transform into good? If so, why? Was he powerless to turn and transform all matter so that no evil remained, even though God is omnipotent? (7.5.7)

This passage not only states the Consistency Problem of Evil; it also rejects two solutions to the problem, one of which Augustine continued to find attractive. One possible solution is to say that evil does not come from the omnipotent Creator, but from the matter the Creator had to use in creating the world. Augustine never found this solution attractive, partly because he supposes that God created the heavens and the earth out of nothing. Augustine was willing to suppose that God first created formless matter out of nothing, and then created the world out of that formless matter. But by supposing that God created formless matter, Augustine removed the plausibility of saying that an all-good, all-powerful God might have been unable to create creatures uninfected with evil because of the evil of matter.

The solution mentioned in T4 that Augustine continued to find attractive makes use of the Neoplatonic doctrine that evil is privation or lack, literally, nonbeing. He returns to that solution a little later in Book 7 of the *Confessions*:

> T5. It was obvious to me that things which are liable to corruption are good. If they were the supreme goods, or if they were not good at all, they could not be corrupted. For if they were supreme goods, they would be incorruptible. If there were no good in them, there would be nothing capable of being corrupted . . . If they were to exist and to be immune from corruption, they would be superior because they would be permanently incorruptible. What could be more absurd than to say that by losing all good, things are made better? So then, if they are deprived of all good, they will be nothing at all. Therefore as long as they exist, they are good. Accordingly, whatever things exist are good, and the evil into whose origins I was inquiring is not a substance . . . (7.12.18)

Yet this is not Augustine's primary response to the Consistency Problem of Evil. Before we consider his primary response, however, we should return to the problem itself and reflect a little more on the challenge it poses.

As I have already pointed out, Hume considers that the three statements whose conjunction is supposed to form the Consistency Problem constitute an inconsistent triad. But when we think about it, we can see that the conjunction 'God is all-good and God is all-powerful and there is evil' is not formally inconsistent. That is, it does not, as stated, logically entail anything of the form 'p and not p.' Why should Hume, or anyone else, have thought otherwise? The answer must be that one automatically supplies an additional premise, something that seems obviously true and hardly in need of stating. There are various ways that one could formulate this additional "Bridge Premise," as I shall call it. Here is one way:

(4) If there were a being that is both all-good and all-powerful, there would be no evil.

The idea behind (4) is that no all-good being would want there to be any evil at all, and so, if this being were also all-powerful, it would make sure that no evil existed.

The conjunction of (1), (2), (3), and (4) is indeed logically, or formally, inconsistent. But we need to reflect a moment on the status of (4). We have added it as an assumed premise. But how do we know it is true? It is clearly not an empirical claim, or a generalization about the all-good and all-powerful beings we know of. If it is true, it must be some sort of conceptual truth.

Is (4) really and truly a conceptual truth? To reject an allegedly conceptual truth, all we need do is show that, *conceivably*, it is false. Thus to reject (4) in such a way as to defeat the Consistency Problem of Evil, all we need show is

(5) Conceivably, it is not the case that (4).

In other words, all we need show is this:

(6) It is conceivable that there would be evil even if there existed an all-good and all-powerful being.

To show (6) to be true all we would need to establish is that an all-good and all-powerful being *might have* a sufficient reason to allow the existence of evil.

What could that sufficient reason be? One of Augustine's answers is that evil comes into the world through free human choice. In recent literature on the Consistency Problem of Evil, this type of solution is called, following Alvin Plantinga, the "Free Will Defense."[3] The idea is that without free human choice we human beings would not be able to be morally good. As Augustine sometimes puts it, having free choice of the will is an intermediate good. It allows for human goodness. But of course, it also allows for human beings to act wrongly and so to introduce evil into the world. God, even in his all-powerfulness and all-goodness, cannot, according to the Free Will Defense, create the possibility of the moral goodness of His creatures without also introducing the possibility of evil.

So how does Augustine's Free Will Defense respond to the Consistency Problem of Evil? To support (6), we offer this consideration:

(7) Even an all-good and all-powerful being might have a sufficient reason to allow evil to exist.

To back up (7) we offer this:

(8) Any possible world in which there are human beings with free will is better than any possible world in which human beings lack free will

together with this:

(9) It is conceivable that there is no possible world in which there are human beings with free will and no evil.

The conjunction of (8) and (9) amounts to what seems to be a sufficient reason for even an all-good and all-powerful being to allow evil in the world, which satisfies (7). And (7), in turn, makes (6) plausible.

In Book 2 of *On Free Choice of the Will* Augustine distinguishes three classes of goods, as follows:

> T6. The virtues, by which we live rightly, are great goods, while all kinds of physical beauty, without which we can live rightly, are the lowest goods. The powers of the spirit, without which no one can live rightly, are the intermediate goods between these two. No one uses the virtues for evil. However, the other goods, the lowest and intermediate ones, can be used not only for good, but also for evil. (2.50.191–2)

Augustine tries in several passages to explain why it is that free will is an intermediate good. Taking our cue from T6, we may suspect that free will counts as a "power of the spirit without which no one can live rightly." What Augustine means by that claim becomes clearer in Book 3, for example, when Evodius says this, apparently with Augustine's concurrence:

> T7. Since, indeed, a good God made me, I cannot do any good except by my will. It is quite clear that a good God gave me the will for this purpose. If the movement by which the will is turned this way and that were not voluntary and within our power, we could not be praised when we turn to higher things, or blamed when, as if on a pivot, we turn toward lower ones. (3.1.3.12–13)

It seems clear to Augustine that the fact that there are moral agents, capable of doing both good and evil, is good. This passage later in Book 3 of *On Free Choice of the Will* makes that clear:

> T8. Just as a stray horse is better than a stone which is not astray, since the stone does not have its own motion or perception, so the creature who sins of his own free will is more excellent than the creature who does not sin because he has no free will. (3.5.15.57)

So this is Augustine's Free Will Defense.

The Free Will Defense is not Augustine's only way of disarming the Consistency Problem of Evil. Another way, as I have already mentioned, is to deny the substantial existence of evil by appeal to the Neoplatonic idea that evil is a deficiency, or lack. Only God is perfectly good, according to this reasoning. If there is to be anything besides God, this reasoning continues, it must be imperfect. In creating human beings God created things that, because they are not God, are imperfect and therefore evil. What God creates is, however, in its own way good, but, being imperfect, also evil. Let us call this the "Imperfection Solution" to the Consistency Problem of Evil.

The Imperfection Solution rejects the bridge principle with the claim that even an all-good all-powerful being could not create something distinct from itself that is perfect, and therefore free from evil. Here is a passage from Augustine's *Enchiridion* in which he sketches the Imperfection Solution to the Consistency Problem of Evil:

> T9. All things that exist, therefore, seeing that the Creator of them all is supremely good, are themselves good. But because they are not, like their Creator, supremely and unchangeably good, their good may be diminished and increased. But for good to be diminished is an evil, although, however much it may be diminished, it is necessary, if the being is to continue, that some good should remain to constitute the being. (12)

And here is a related passage from Book 7 of the *Confessions*:

> T10. It was obvious to me that things which are liable to corruption are good. If they were supreme goods, or if they were not good at all, they could not be corrupted. (7.12.18)

There is also in Augustine a third solution to the Consistency Problem of Evil. We can call it the "Necessary Contrast Solution." It is expressed in, for example, this passage from Book 11 of the *City of God*:

> T11. If no one had sinned in the world, the world would have been furnished and fitted only with things naturally good. And the fact that sin has happened does not mean that the whole universe is full of sin, since by far the greater number of celestial bodies preserve the order of their nature; and the evil will that refused to keep to the order did not for that reason escape the laws of God who orders all things well. A picture may be beautiful when it has touches of black in appropriate places; in the same way the whole universe is beautiful, if one could see it as a whole, even with its sinners, though their ugliness is disgusting when they are viewed in themselves. (11.23)

Augustine does not say in T11 that there could be no good without evil. He does say that the whole universe can have a beauty that encompasses the good and the bad, just as a beautiful picture may have dark areas as well as light ones. Perhaps this point is meant to fit together with the Privation Solution. Since any creation will be less than perfect, the only way for the creation to be beautiful will be for its privations to be ordered in an appropriate way. Thus even an all-good and all-powerful being could not create a perfect creation. The most such a being could do is to create a world in which imperfections are ordered in such a way as to highlight the good. This conclusion might then give further support to (6).

Is any one of Augustine's solutions to the Consistency Problem of Evil satisfactory? Thanks to the work of Alvin Plantinga and others, it is, I think, the Free Will Defense that has received the most thorough recent discussion. Central to this recent discussion has been the question of whether God could have given human beings free choice of the will but made them such that they would always make the morally correct choices. Plantinga has mounted an impressive argument for concluding that, possibly, God, even though an all-good and all-powerful being, could not have actualized a world in which there is the moral goodness, which requires human freedom, but no evil. Here is part of Plantinga's conclusion:

> God can create a world containing moral good only by creating significantly free persons. And, since every person is the instantiation of an essence, he can create significantly free persons only by instantiating some creaturely essences. But if every such essence suffers from transworld depravity, then no matter which essences God instantiated, the resulting persons, if free with respect to morally significant actions, would always perform some wrong actions. If every creaturely essence suffers from transworld depravity, then it was beyond the power of God himself to create a world containing moral good but no moral evil.[4]

Although Plantinga has made use of an idea of individual essences not to be found in Augustine, as well as a sophisticated modal semantics unavailable to Augustine, his conclusion seems to accord in a general way with Augustine's own Free Will Defense.

There is, however, a way in which Augustine's own views on heaven seem to undermine his Free Will Defense. In Book 22 of the *City of God* Augustine tells us that those of us who make it to heaven will be unable to delight in sin. In a way that inability seems to be a great blessing. But it may also seem to be a loss. What about the free will of the blessed in heaven? Here is Augustine's reply:

> T12. Now the fact that they will be unable to delight in sin does not entail that they will have no free will. In fact, the will will be freer, in that it is freed from a delight in sin and immovably fixed in a delight in not sinning. The first freedom of will, given to man when he was created upright at the beginning, was an ability not to sin, combined with the possibility of sinning. But this last freedom will be more potent, for it will bring the impossibility of sinning; yet this also will be the result of God's gift, not of some inherent quality of nature. For to be a partaker of God is not the same thing as to be God; the inability to sin belongs to God's nature, while he who partakes of God's nature receives the impossibility of sinning as a gift from

God. Moreover, the stages of the divine gift had to be preserved. Free will was given first, with the ability to sin; and the last gift was the inability to sin. The first freedom was designed for acquiring merit; the last gift was concerned with the reception of a reward. (22.30)

Surprisingly, according to this passage, it is possible to have free will and, at the same time, not just successfully resist every temptation to sin, but actually be unable to sin! Of course it is only by the grace of God that the elect will have freedom of the will and, at the same time, the inability to sin. But, Augustine says, it is only by the grace of God that any one of us has free will in the first place. So why could God not, by His grace, have given Adam, and all the rest of us, freedom of the will together with the inability to sin? Augustine does say that "the first freedom was designed for acquiring merit." Yet he, more than any other prominent Christian, rejects the idea that we can merit salvation. So why is it important for human beings to be able to acquire merit?

Augustine seems to be in a bind. His Free Will Defense requires that, conceivably, even an all-good and all-powerful being could not allow human beings to be free agents without allowing evil to exist. Yet his idea of the second Divine gift of freedom has God giving the elect in heaven a higher kind of freedom that includes an inability to sin.

Here is the bind. As I set up the Consistency Problem of Evil I pointed out that the conjunction of (1), (2), and (3) is not a formal contradiction. I said we would need a Bridge Premise to yield a formal contradiction. I suggested this premise:

(4) If there were a being that is both all-good and all-powerful, there would be no evil.

I added that (4) would need to be a conceptual truth, so that all we would need to defeat the claim of inconsistency would be to make this claim plausible:

(6) It is conceivable that there would be evil even if there existed an all-good and all-powerful being.

The Free Will Defense supports (6) by making this claim plausible:

(7) Even an all-good and all-powerful being might have a sufficient reason to allow evil to exist.

A crucial part of making (7) plausible is this claim:

(9) It is conceivable that there is no possible world in which there are human beings with free will and there is no evil.

Augustine's thoughts about the "the last gift" of free will call (9) into question. It seems that if what Augustine says about the free will of the elect in heaven is at all plausible, God could have made Adam and Eve with free will, indeed with a higher kind of freedom, yet without even the possibility of their choosing to eat the apple.

This brings us back to the question raised by J. L. Mackie, among others, that initiated the recent discussion of the Consistency Problem of Evil:

> T13. If God has made men such that in their free choices they sometimes prefer what is good and sometimes what is evil, why could he not have made men such that they always freely choose the good?[5]

In view of Augustine's discussion of free will in heaven, I must admit that I do not see how he can answer the challenge of T13 in a satisfactory way.

further reading

Alvin Plantinga, *The Nature of Necessity*. Oxford: Clarendon Press, 1974, ch. 9, "God, evil, and the metaphysics of freedom." Plantinga's reasoning on the Consistency Problem of Evil has motivated much of the recent discussion of this problem.

notes

1 David Hume, *Dialogues Concerning Natural Religion*, pt. 10.
2 *Confessions* 3.5.9.
3 Alvin Plantinga, *God and Other Minds* (Ithaca: Cornell University Press, 1967), ch. 6, "The free will defense."
4 Alvin Plantinga, *The Nature of Necessity* (Oxford: Clarendon Press, 1974), pp. 188–9.
5 J. L. Mackie, "Evil and omnipotence," *Mind* 64 (1955): 209.

wanting bad things

In a famous passage in one of Plato's dialogues (*Meno* 77b), the character Meno is made to suggest that virtue is (i) wanting noble things (*ta kala*) and (ii) having the power to acquire them. Socrates gets Meno to agree that by 'noble things' he simply means good things. Then Socrates asks, in seeming bafflement, whether Meno thinks that, although some people want good things, others actually want bad things. His point is that, unless, conceivably, some people actually do want bad things, the first half of Meno's suggestion as to the nature of virtue, namely, wanting good (or noble) things, will be empty and so will not play any role in marking off virtue from nonvirtue.

Meno, for his part, thinks it obvious that some people do want bad things. But Socrates presses him hard by drawing a distinction: "Do you mean," Socrates asks Meno, "that some people want bad things believing them to be good, or is it that some people want bad things knowing them to be bad?" (77c). "Both," replies Meno, simply.

Socrates expends very little effort in the dialogue trying to show that nobody wants bad things, thinking that they are good. His idea seems to be that if one mistakenly supposes that an object of desire is good, when it is really bad, then the real object of one's desire is not the actually bad object one *seems* to want, but rather the good object one has pictured for oneself.

What, now, about the other kind of case that Socrates identifies? Can we ever want bad things, knowing that they are bad, or even believing that they are bad? Here Socrates assumes that my wanting bad things, if it were possible, would be my wanting things that it would be bad for me to get. Thus, he seems to reason, my wanting bad things *believing* them to be bad would be wanting them *believing* that they would be bad for me to get. (We might wish to question that inference.) Getting bad things, he adds, would be getting harmful things that would make one miserable. Socrates gets Meno to agree that no one wants to be harmed or made miserable.

Here all sorts of complications set in. Can I want another smoke, knowing that, *in the long run*, smoking is bad for me even if, in the short run, I would enjoy the pleasure of a smoke? Surely I can. Socrates does not discuss this kind of case in the Meno. But we can easily imagine what he would say: Doing such a thing would only be possible by putting out of one's mind the long-term badness and focusing on the short-term goodness, which would then be the true object of one's desire.

Perhaps I have said enough about the *Meno* passage to make clear that Socratic reasoning can easily lead us to conclude that wanting bad things requires either ignoring or else simply being ignorant in some crucial way about the badness of what one wants. That conclusion fits well with the Socratic idea that virtue is a kind of knowledge and that vice, wanting what are, in fact, bad things, is a kind of ignorance. That idea is made plausible by the somewhat more general thought that one could not want a thing except by thinking that it would be, in some way or other, a good thing to do or have. One wants whatever one wants, it is sometimes put, "under the form of the Good" – that is, conceived as something good. Let's call this thesis "(W1)" and formulate it in the following way:

(W1) Wanting something is always wanting something one believes at the time to be good.

Augustine seems to have been the first important philosopher to question (W1). He does this by telling a rather ordinary story about a prank he participated in as an adolescent. Before he tells the story, however, he explains a bit about the context. In his *Confessions*, he writes, "During my sixteenth year there was an interruption in my studies. I was recalled from Madauros, the nearby town where I had first lived away from home to learn literature and oratory. During that time funds were gathered in preparation for a more distant absence at Carthage, for which my father had more enthusiasm than cash, since he was a citizen of Thagaste with very modest resources" (2.3.5).

Finding himself on a sort of extended holiday before being sent off for higher education in Carthage, Augustine did things he would later regret. Looking back on this year three decades later, when he wrote his *Confessions*, he could say:

T1. At one time in adolescence I was burning to find satisfaction in hellish pleasures. I ran wild in the shadowy jungle of erotic adventures. (2.1.1)

Augustine describes this year as one of idleness in which he began to "show signs of virility and the stirrings of adolescence" (2.3.6). "Among my peer group," he writes, "I was ashamed not to be equally guilty of shameful behavior when I heard them boasting of their sexual exploits" (2.3.7). He continues:

T2. Such were the companions with whom I made my way through the streets of Babylon. With them I rolled in its dung as if rolling in spices and precious ointments...The reins were relaxed to allow me to amuse myself. There was no strict discipline to keep me in check, which led to an unbridled dissoluteness in many different directions. (2.3.8)

With a buildup like T1 and T2 we might expect a story in which Augustine disgraces his family by making the underage daughter of a local landowner pregnant. But what follows is something very different. Here is the story that forms the centerpiece of *Confessions* 2:

T3. There was a pear tree near our vineyard laden with fruit, though attractive in neither colour nor taste. To shake the fruit off the tree and carry off the pears a gang of naughty adolescents and I set off late at night after (in our usual pestilential way) we had continued our game in the streets. We carried off a huge load of pears. But they were not for our feasts but merely to throw to the pigs. Even if we ate a few, nevertheless our pleasure lay in doing what was not allowed. (2.4.9)

This incident seems somehow too ordinary to be the focus of a whole book of Augustine's *Confessions*. Yet Augustine invests it with great significance. In this theft, he writes:

T4. I became evil for no reason. I had no motive for my wickedness except the wickedness itself. It was foul, and I loved it. I loved the self-destruction, I loved my fall, not the object for which I had fallen but my fall itself. My depraved soul leaped down from your firmament to ruin. I was seeking not to gain anything by shameful means, but shame for its own sake. (2.4.9)

It is difficult to take the rhetoric of this passage seriously. Yet Augustine seems to want us to do so. He seems to be deadly serious when he claims that
(a) he became evil for no reason;
(b) his motive was to achieve wickedness;
(c) what he did was foul and he loved it; and
(d) he was seeking to do something shameful for the sake of doing something shameful.
There could hardly be a more emphatic rejection of (W1) than this.
Augustine seems to realize that we readers will be baffled by his account of his motivation in stealing the pears. How can we be expected to believe that anybody would become evil for no reason, or that Augustine's motive was to achieve wickedness, or that he loved what was foul, or that he was seeking to do something shameful for the sake of doing something shameful? How could anyone believe such claims?

Somewhat surprisingly, Augustine begins his attempt to make his motivation comprehensible by talking about beauty. Thus T4 is followed immediately by this:

> T5. There is beauty in lovely physical objects as in gold and silver and all other such things. When the body touches such things, much significance attaches to the rapport of the object with the touch. Each of the other senses has its own appropriate mode of response to physical things. Temporal honour and the power of giving orders and of being in command have their own kind of dignity, though this is also the origin of self-assertion. (2.5.10)

What is going on here? First Augustine gives a baffling account of his motivation for stealing pears with his adolescent gang. Then he starts talking about beauty. How is beauty relevant to understanding the pear episode?

The relevance of beauty, I suggest, is this. Often we can explain why some person, A, chose to φ by making clear how A could think of φing itself, or what A might hope to get by φing, as beautiful, or, at the very least, as attractive. For example, most of us think gold and silver and things made of them are beautiful. We can understand that someone who sees an unguarded gold or silver cup might want to steal it. The implicit thesis here is something like this:

(W2) If A chooses to φ, then, other things being equal, the fact (if it is a fact) that A thinks φing is an attractive thing to do, or else thinks φing is a good way to get some attractive object, explains why A chooses to φ.

If Augustine can make clear how he could think stealing is an attractive thing to do, or else that stealing is a good way to get some attractive object, then he has, other things being equal, an explanation for why he chose to steal.

Augustine goes on to say this:

> T6. The life which we live in this world has its attractiveness because of a certain measure in its beauty and its harmony with all these inferior objects that are beautiful. (2.5.10)

The mention of inferior objects that are, nevertheless, beautiful in their own way, invites us to consider whether a wrongful act might be understood as an agent's being attracted to something that has its own beauty, even though its beauty is outshone by that of an alternative, but superior, object. Augustine writes:

T7. When a crime is under investigation to discover the motive for which it was done, the accusation is not usually believed except in cases where the appetite to obtain (or the fear of losing) one of those goods which we have called inferior appears a plausible possibility. They are beautiful and attractive even if, in comparison with the higher goods which give true happiness, they are mean and base. (2.5.11)

Even the actions of that most wicked Roman emperor, Cataline, Augustine tells us, can be understood as motivated by an attraction to lesser goods, and objects of inferior beauty:

T8. It was said of one brutal and cruel man [Cataline] that he was evil and savage without reason. Yet the preceding passage gave the motive: "Lest disuse might make his hand or mind slow to react." . . . His objective was to capture the city by violent crimes to obtain honors, government, and wealth. . . . No, not even Cataline himself loved his crimes; something else motivated him to commit them. (2.5.11)

So does the example of the evil and wicked Cataline help Augustine to understand his own sinful act? Apparently not. Addressing his act of theft as if it were another person he says:

T9. There was nothing beautiful about you [my act of theft] (2.6.12)

Adding to his puzzlement Augustine draws on his understanding of evil as a deficiency, a mere "nothing," to ask, plaintively, "Do you exist at all for me to be addressing you?"

The pears he stole, Augustine concedes, were beautiful as being part of God's creation. But, he insists, it was not really the pears that he was attracted to. He had better ones at home. The ones he picked, he tells us, he picked solely with the motive of stealing. He threw the pears themselves away. "My feasting," he goes on, "was only on the wickedness which I took pleasure in enjoying" (2.6.12). But wickedness, it seems, cannot be understood as a lesser good with its own beauty. And Augustine makes no effort to get us to conceive it that way.

At the very end of this section Augustine tells us that vice is sometimes a "flawed reflection of beauty" (2.6.12). What he means by that comment is presumably brought out in the next section. "Pride imitates what is lofty," he tells us, "but you alone are God most high above all things" (2.6.13). Augustine then goes on to produce a list of what he seems to consider vices, including ambition, cruelty, soft endearments, and [mere] curiosity. The point of this list seems to be summed up in the next section, where Augustine tells us, "In their perverted way all humanity imitates you" (2.6.14). That observation leads Augustine into a line of explanation that he seems to accept. Addressing God, he says this:

T10. In their perverted way all humanity imitates you. Yet they put themselves at a distance from you and exalt themselves against you. But even
by thus imitating you they acknowledge that you are the creator of all
nature and concede that there is no place where one can entirely escape
from you. Therefore in that act of theft what was the object of my love,
and in what way did I viciously and perversely imitate my Lord? Was my
pleasure to break your law, but by deceit, since I had not the power to do
that by force? Was I acting like a prisoner with restricted liberty who
does with impunity what is not permitted, thereby making an assertion
of possessing a dim resemblance to omnipotence? Was it possible to take
pleasure in what was not allowed for no other reason than that it was not
allowed? (2.6.14)

Here we have the picture of a prisoner who, frustrated and resentful at
being under the rule of another, acts as if free from constraint in a futile
effort to prove his freedom. The prisoner's action is, in a way, perfectly
understandable. Perhaps we ourselves have on occasion acted in futile
defiance of a parent or teacher or other authority figure. Although understandable, the action may be irrational in that it has no chance of changing the power relationship. The action may also be self-destructive, even
deliberately self-destructive. Since it seeks no worthwhile goal, it is
nihilistic. Let us call a person who acts out of this sort of motivation a
"Rebel Without a Cause," after the movie of that name starring James
Dean.

The Rebel Without a Cause wants to perform an action without believing either that the action, or what the action may achieve, is either
good or beautiful. Thus the Rebel Without a Cause is a counterexample
to (W1). Moreover the Rebel's action does not fall under the explanatory
schema (W2). This Rebel acts, not even according to a Nietzschean trans-
valuation of values, but simply from resentment and frustration.

So here, at last, we have a somewhat plausible explanation of Augustine's theft. Perhaps he was rebelling, in a futile and foolish way, against
God and God's morality. His theft was, perhaps the act of a perverted
will.

In the final stage of his argument, Augustine turns to what at first
glance may seem to be a much more satisfying explanation. He was,
after all, taking part in a gang action. Maybe what Augustine sought was
the camaraderie of the gang. Augustine writes:

T11. What fruit had I, wretched boy, in these things which I now blush to
recall, above all in that theft in which I loved nothing but the theft itself?
The theft itself was a nothing, and for that reason, I was the more miserable. Yet had I been alone, I would not have done it – I remember my state
of mind to be thus at the time – alone I would never have done it. Therefore
my love in that act was to be associated with the gang in whose company

I did it. Does it follow that I loved something other than the theft? No, nothing else in reality because association with the gang is also a nothing. (2.8.16)

This is a difficult passage to interpret. But Augustine seems here to commit himself to these claims:

(C1) In his act of theft, he loved nothing but the act of theft itself.
(C2) What he loved in that act of theft was to be associated with the gang.
(C3) He would not have performed the act of theft except in the company of others.
(C4) Yet he loved nothing other than the theft.

(C2) and (C4) seem to be in direct conflict. I shall try to show, a little later, how we might try to resolve that apparent conflict.

We might have expected that Augustine would supplant his suggestion about the Rebel Without a Cause with the explanation that he acted out of a desire to be approved by the gang. But what he does is something different from that. For one thing, he never withdraws his insistence that his pleasure lay in committing the act itself. Here is part of the next section, in which he elaborates on (C2) and (C3):

T12. Had I been alone, it would have given me absolutely no pleasure, nor would I have committed [the act]. Friendship can be a dangerous enemy, a seduction of the mind lying beyond the reach of investigation. Out of a game and a jest came an avid desire to do injury and an appetite to inflict loss on someone else without any motive of personal gain on my part, and no pleasure in settling a score. As soon as the words are spoken, "Let's go and do it", one is ashamed not to be shameless. (2.9.17)

But T12 does more than elaborate on (C2) and (C3). It adds these claims:

(C5) He would not have taken pleasure in the act of theft, if he had been alone.
(C6) He had an avid desire to do injury and an appetite to inflict loss on someone else without any motive of personal gain on his part, and no pleasure in settling a score.

Can any sense be made of the conjunction of (C1) through (C6)? For starters we might think of mob actions, for example, lynchings, or gang rapes. It may very well be that many members of a given gang seek the approval or admiration of other gang members. But perhaps some participants in, say, a gang rape, find that the effect of acting in a gang is primarily, or even solely, to remove their inhibitions and free them to assault an innocent woman without other cause or motive except the sadistic desire to assault a woman. It may also be especially exhilarating to act in consort with others. What I have in mind is not that the gang member is seeking the approval of the others. It is rather that the group action, in which the individual is participating has a special thrill it would not have if the individual were acting alone.

If we want to see mob evil on a large screen, we might think of the horrendous horrors of the twentieth century – the Holocaust, the killing fields of Cambodia, the massacres of Rwanda. No doubt the motivation of individuals who participated in those horrors were often very complicated and very diverse. But these examples of mass evil seem to illustrate the point that mob action unleashes motivational forces that go well beyond wanting to be accepted or admired by the mob. And at least sometimes, it seems plausible to say that the atrocities are committed for the sake of committing atrocities, even though the participants would not have committed such atrocities on their own.

Of course a gang's theft of some pears is relatively insignificant in comparison with a gang rape, let alone a massacre. Yet the motivational structure of vast horrors may be mirrored in something as tame as stealing some pears from someone against whom one has no grudge, and then throwing those pears willfully to the swine.

So here is my suggestion as to how Augustine understands his act of theft. First, he leaves standing his "perversion account," the Rebel Without a Cause. He was throwing over the traces of God's morality, but without substituting for it any new morality of his own.

Augustine then supplements the Rebel story with an account of mob action. In concert with the gang he did something he would never have done on his own. But he does not see himself as acting so as to receive the approval or admiration of the gang. What he loved was the act itself, but performed in concert with the gang.

In the coda to *Confessions* 2, the very last section, which is only a short paragraph, Augustine does two more things. First he expresses exasperation at his own best attempt to understand his theft. He writes:

> T13. Who can untie this extremely twisted and tangled knot? It is a foul affair, I have no wish to give attention to it; I have no desire to contemplate it. (2.10.18)

Then, in the very last sentence of Book 2, he makes this summary judgment on his moral and religious state at the time of this theft:

> T14. I became to myself a region of destitution.

I take T13 to express Augustine's lingering perplexity about his action and his dissatisfaction with his best efforts to understand it. Something like this is a feature of the horrors of the twentieth century. We are puzzled and perplexed at how people who, before their participation in, say, a great massacre, can seem to be, indeed, can be, such ordinary people. They are the person next door. Even more scarily, they are me! How did such ordinary, seemingly decent people, come to participate in such horrendous acts of evil? It boggles the mind. We want to say with Augustine, "Who can untie this extremely twisted and tangled knot?"

It is interesting to me that Joel Feinberg, in a recent discussion of evil, claims that such perplexity is partly constitutive of what he calls "pure evil." Feinberg writes:

> The purely evil wrongdoer may be taken by surprise by his own voluntary action. His conduct will seem mysterious to other people and likely will remain mysterious even after extensive study. If his conduct . . . remains a mystery, it may remain a mystery to *him* as well as to everybody else. His harmful action, having no motive intelligible to him or to anyone else, was done for no apparent reason and seems even to him to be incomprehensible. That must be what pure evil feels like from the inside. At its best, it is an astonishingly opaque phenomenon. At its worst it is, well, plain evil, nothing more, nothing less.[1]

I take T14 to express Augustine's anguish, both at his recognition that gang action can bring out such profound evil in him, and that he had at this time no real moral moorings. He was a Rebel Without a Cause. Without any effective moral moorings he was able to have "an avid desire to do injury and an appetite to inflict loss on someone else" without cause.

I suggest that the graphic portrayals of evil available to us today on our living-room TV sets should prepare us to find in Augustine's account of an adolescent escapade a small but clear window into the dark recesses of the human psyche. Through that window we can perhaps see that a not unusually evil person might sometimes do wrong just for the pleasure of doing wrong, especially when that wrongdoing is done in exhilarating concert with others.

There is a final paradox and perversity about the act Augustine has focused his attention on. Although that act is a counterexample to (W1) and stubbornly resists falling under the explanatory schema (W2), the very opacity of the act, to use Feinberg's expression, is a tribute to the attractiveness and plausibility of (W1) and (W2). We naturally seek to understand an action as something that the actor, at least at the time of action, believed to be a good thing to do. When we have to confront an action that resists being understood in that way, we naturally respond with Augustinian despair: "Who can untie this extremely twisted and tangled knot? It is a foul affair, I have no wish to give attention to it; I have no desire to contemplate it."

further reading

Scott MacDonald, "Petit larceny, the beginning of all sin: Augustine's theft of the pears," *Faith and Philosophy* 20 (2003): 393–414. This article presents a very different interpretation of *Confessions* 2.

note

1 Joel Feinberg, *Problems at the Roots of Law* (New York: Oxford University Press, 2003), p. 150.

lying

N ear the end of Book 3 of Plato's *Republic*, Socrates explains that, in the ideal city-state he is describing, it will be necessary to tell the citizenry a noble or royal lie.

"What sort of lie?" Glaucon asks. (414b)

Socrates then concocts a tall tale that is supposed to convince everyone that the "gold people," those who have shown by aptitude tests that they are best suited to rule, must be the rulers, that the "silver people," those who have been shown to have the required aptitude for soldiering, should make up the army, and that the "brass and iron people" must be the artisans. Included in the tall tale is a story about how the time adult citizens spent as youths was actually a dream. In reality they were formed of their respective metals in the earth and brought forth to play the roles in society their particular make-up suits them for.

Glaucon is skeptical that citizens will believe this "noble lie," at least not in the first generation. Socrates allows that it may take more than one generation for the tall tale to be accepted. But he insists that the effort to get it accepted will make citizens care for each other and for the city.

We today are well aware of the evil that has been wrought by stories of racial and ethnic superiority and inferiority. And we are all too familiar with the baleful effect of government propaganda and social stereotyping. It is profoundly unsettling to find that Plato, one of the greatest philosophers of all time, should have advocated a state-sponsored lie to promote social cohesion and the acceptance of unequal power relationships within the city-state.

Yet Plato's advocacy of lying, when it serves the well-being of the society, should not come as a great surprise. No Platonic dialogue is devoted to the analysis of the virtue of honesty. In fact, honesty is not included among any of the lists of moral virtues in the Platonic dialogues.

Back in Book 2 of the *Republic* Plato has Socrates take a purely consequentialist position on telling lies. He asks Adeimantus:

What about falsehood in words? When and to whom is it useful and so not deserving of hatred? Isn't it useful against one's enemies? And when any of our so-called friends are attempting, through madness or ignorance, to do something bad, isn't it a useful drug for preventing them? It is also useful in the case of those stories we were just talking about, the ones we tell because we don't know the truth about those ancient events involving the gods. By making a falsehood as much like the truth as we can, don't we also make it useful? (382cd)

Adeimantus agrees.

Socrates goes on to contrast the occasional usefulness of telling lies for a human being with the necessary honesty of a god. "A god, then, is simple and true in word and deed," Socrates says. "He doesn't change himself or deceive others by images, words, or signs, whether in visions or in dreams" (382e).

So, in a way, Plato does recognize truthfulness as a virtue. It is a virtue that a god has. Yet, apparently, it is not something that human beings need aspire to.

Aristotle discusses truthfulness (*alētheia*) as a virtue in his *Nicomachean Ethics*, although not prominently. He seems to think of truthfulness as sincerity, as opposed to boastfulness on the one hand, and deceptive understatement on the other. But he never takes on the task of trying to say what it is to tell a lie. Apparently that project never struck him as a significant philosophical challenge.

In fact, the concept of what it is to tell a lie is philosophically very problematic. Surprisingly, no philosopher of antiquity seems to have realized this. One possible explanation for this neglect is the fact that honesty seems not to have been an especially prominent virtue in classical Greek culture.

Lying is, however, a prominent topic in Judaism and Christianity. The Ninth Commandment, "Thou shalt not bear false witness against thy neighbor" (Exodus 20:16), has been understood to forbid the telling of lies. Lying is forbidden by God in the Old Testament book of Leviticus (19:11) and in the New Testament letter to the Ephesians: "Wherefore putting away lying, speak every man truth with his neighbor" (4:25). It is therefore not surprising that Augustine, the first really great Christian theologian and philosopher, should have written two treatises on lying.

Augustine, in fact, considers all lies sinful. That may not come as a complete surprise. What may be surprising, however, is that Augustine finds the concept of a lie philosophically perplexing. He is, so far as I know, the first philosopher to realize how philosophically problematic the notion of telling a lie really is.

I sometimes ask students in a philosophy class to help me analyze the concept of telling a lie. I put on the board what is to be analyzed, namely:

In saying that p to A, S tells a lie if, and only if, . . .

"What," I ask my students, "are the individually necessary and jointly sufficient conditions for S to lie to A by saying that p?"

Thinking, quite naturally, of a lie as a falsehood, some student will suggest as one necessary condition, 'It is false that p.' I write it on the board.

"But suppose I tell you somebody is waiting for you outside, just to get you out of the room, when, unknown to me, somebody really is outside the room?" some student may ask.

We discuss the example. Most students agree that you meant to tell a lie, to get me out of the room, but what you said was not really a lie. But if the first condition is satisfied, that is, if what one said is really false, we still need to add this second condition: 'S believes that it is false that p.'

"Don't you have to mean to deceive someone with what you are saying?" someone may suggest. There then may follow a rather long discussion of whether intended deception is a necessary condition for telling a lie. I have to admit that I sometimes hear people say, "I lied to you," when all they mean is that what they said was false. That sort of usage discounts the idea that to tell a lie I must believe that what I say is false. But it also ignores any sort of requirement that the speaker intended to deceive the hearer.

My class and I may have a difficult time agreeing on necessary and sufficient conditions for telling a lie. In fact, we usually do. In the end, however, a majority will likely agree on what I shall call the "Standard Analysis":

Standard Analysis

In saying to A that p, S tells a lie if and only if
 (i) it is false that p;
 (ii) S believes that it is false that p; and
 (iii) in saying to A that p, S intends to deceive A about whether p.

These conditions are meant to be individually necessary and jointly sufficient for there to be a genuine case of telling a lie. That is, no case will count as a lie unless it satisfies each of these three conditions. Moreover, any case that satisfies all three will automatically count as telling a lie. Let us call the first condition of the Standard Analysis the "Falsity Condition," the second, the "Believes-False Condition," and the third, the "Deception Condition."

In my class I may point out that self-deception is often characterized as lying to oneself. The idea of lying to oneself, however, presents a serious challenge to the Standard Analysis. Most obviously we will have trouble understanding how one could seriously intend to deceive oneself. It seems that any attempt I might make to get myself to believe something I do not believe by telling myself the opposite of what I really believe is doomed to failure. One could even say that the project of doing that seems incoherent.

We need not, however, go into the especially troubling case of lying to oneself to become perplexed about what it is to tell a lie. In any case, Augustine does not discuss the possibility of lying to oneself. And he finds, quite correctly, I think, that there are many aspects of interpersonal lying that are problematic enough to engage our philosophical skills. He, too, seems to be tempted to accept the Standard Analysis. But he thinks of enough cases that he is inclined to call cases of lying that do not fit the Standard Analysis to make his discussion of lying an exemplary piece of philosophy.

Augustine's interest in what it is to tell a lie has at least two sources. One is the Ninth Commandment, which I have already mentioned. But another source is the saying of Jesus "I am the way, the truth, and the light; no one comes to the Father but by me" (John 14:6). This seems to Augustine to rule out any "noble lie." Lying, for whatever motive, is seen by him as a barrier to reaching God.

Augustine wrote two treatises on the topic of lying, *On Lying* (*De mendacio*) and *Against Lying* (*Contra mendacium*). The first one, written in 395, in the year in which he was consecrated Bishop of Hippo, is the more philosophical of the two. I shall concentrate on it, and especially on the first four chapters. Ironically, Augustine says in his *Reconsiderations* (*Retractations*) at 1.27 that he had been dissatisfied with this work because of its obscure style and had decided not to publish it. Although he later ordered it destroyed, it survived, and, when Augustine learned that it had survived, he decided to let it stand. (It seems that philosophers are not always good judges of the worth of their own works.)

Augustine begins his treatise by excluding jokes and jests from consideration (2.2). Of course, the Deception Condition can be expected to take care of these cases anyway, if we accept the Standard Analysis. In fact, what is said in a play, or as an illustration of some grammatical point, can also be expected to fail the Deception Condition.

In Chapter 3 Augustine affirms the Believes-False Condition. He writes:

> T1. . . . the person who utters a falsehood does not lie if he believes, or, at least, assumes, that what he says is true (3.3)

Augustine embellishes his point this way:

T2. He lies ... who holds one opinion in his mind and who gives expression to another through words or any other outward manifestation. For this reason the heart of a liar is said to be double, that is, twofold in its thinking: one part consisting in that knowledge which he knows or thinks to be true, yet does not so express it; the other part consisting of that knowledge which he knows or thinks to be false, yet expresses as true. (3.3)

At least two things are interesting about T2. One is the idea that one may lie through an "outward manifestation" that is not verbal. Thus, according to Augustine, I can lie by, say, nodding in agreement, or shaking my head in disagreement. I have to say that not all my students are willing to count a nod or other nonverbal sign as a lie.

The second interesting thing about T2 is the suggestion that the "double heart," that is, saying something other than what one believes, may be sufficient for a lie. What emerges a few lines later is not that the Believes-False Condition is by itself sufficient to make a statement count as a lie, but that, coupled with the Deception Condition, it is sufficient. Augustine writes:

T3. Likewise, it happens that a person who is actually lying may say what is true, if he believes that what he says is false, yet offers it as true, even if the actual truth be just what he says. For, a person is to be judged as lying or not lying according to the intention of his own mind, not according to the truth or falsity of the matter itself. He who expresses the false as true because he thinks it to be true may be said to be mistaken or rash, but he cannot, in fairness, be said to be lying, because, when he so expresses himself, he does not have a false heart nor does he wish to deceive; rather, he himself is deceived. (3.3)

What T3 seems to give us is this alternative analysis of lying:

First Alternative Analysis

In saying to A that p, S tells a lie if and only if
 (i) S believes that it is false that p; and
 (ii) in saying to A that p, S intends to deceive A.

Augustine next goes on to a more difficult case:

T4. Let us consider a person who says what he believes is false and what is actually false but with the thought of not being believed, so that in this way, by a kind of false faith, he may deter from action the hearer who, he realizes, will not believe him. (4.4)

The kind of case Augustine describes in T4 seems to be illustrated by the story of the traveling salesman in old Russia who meets his archrival at the train station and asks him where he is going that day.

"To Minsk," replies the rival.

"You're just telling me that you're going to Minsk," says the first salesman, "so that I'll think you're going to Pinsk when *you really are going to Minsk, you dirty liar!*"

Jokes aside, what should we say about someone who tells the truth, thinking that it is in fact the truth, but with the intention of deceiving someone expected to assume that what is said will not be the truth? Can a statement that is the truth be a lie?

Sometimes we mislead others by failing to correct their misunderstandings. But Augustine's Minsk–Pinsk case is different. Something is said that is believed by the speaker to be true and is, in fact, true, but in circumstances in which the speaker can expect the hearer to interpret it as a falsehood. Augustine does not seem to know what to do with this case. I am myself inclined to say it is not a case of lying, both because it fails to satisfy the Believes-False Condition and because it fails to satisfy the Deception Condition. But then I am much more nearly satisfied with the Standard Analysis than Augustine is.

Augustine next considers this case:

> T5. In the first place, we have a person who knows or thinks that he is speaking falsely, yet speaks in this way without the intention of deceiving. Such would be the case of a man who, knowing that a certain road is besieged by bandits and fearing that a friend for whose safety he is concerned will take that road, tells that friend that there are no bandits there. He makes this assertion, realizing that his friend does not trust him, and, because of the statement to the contrary of the person in whom he has no faith, will therefore believe that the bandits are there and will not go by that road. (4.4)

In this case the Falsity Condition is satisfied, and so is the Believes-False Condition. But the Deception Condition is not satisfied. If this person has lied, we have this alternative analysis of lying.

Second Alternative Analysis

In saying to A that *p*, S tells a lie if, and only if,
(i) it is false that *p*; and
(ii) S believes that it is false that *p*.

It is hard to believe that Augustine could be satisfied with the Second Alternative Analysis, since he has emphasized the importance of the "double heart." But I have to say that for some of my students any deliberate statement of a falsehood counts as a lie no matter what intention the speaker has in stating it.

Here is Augustine's next case:

> T6. In the second place, there is the case of the person who knowing or thinking what he says true, nevertheless says it in order to deceive. This would happen if the man mentioned above were to tell his mistrustful acquaintance that there are bandits on that road, knowing that they actually are there and telling it so that his hearer, because of his distrust of the speaker, may proceed to take that road and so fall into the hands of the bandits. (4.4)

If this case counts as a lie, then intent to deceive is itself sufficient for a lie. Thus we have this analysis:

Third Alternative Analysis of Lying

> In saying to A that p S lies if, and only if
> in saying to A that p, S intends to deceive S about whether p.

At this point one might expect Augustine either to settle for the Standard Analysis, or else to go for one of the Alternative Analyses. Instead, this is what he says:

> T7. . . . if a lie is an utterance accompanied by the desire to utter an untruth, he lies who desires to say what is false, and who says what he wishes to say even though it be without the intention to deceive. (4.4)

On a natural reading of T7, Augustine here seems to be appealing to the Second Alternative Analysis of Lying. He continues:

> T8. If, however, a lie is any pronouncement whatsoever if it be accompanied by a desire to deceive, then not the first, but the second, person lies; that is, the one who wishes to deceive even by telling the truth. (4.4)

Here we seem to have an appeal to the Third Alternative Analysis of Lying. Augustine continues:

> T9. But if a lie is an utterance accompanied by the desire of [uttering] any falsity, then both lie, because the first wishes his statement to be false and the second wishes that a false conclusion be drawn from his true statement. (4.4)

This looks like a disjunction of the Second and the Third Analysis. Augustine continues:

> T10. Furthermore, if a lie is the utterance of one who desires to speak untruthfully in order to deceive, then neither one lies, because the former desires to convince a person of the truth by telling what is false and the latter desires to tell the truth so that he may convince a person of what is false. (4.4)

And here we have yet another alternative analysis:

Fourth Alternative Analysis

In saying to A that p S lies if, and only if,
  (i) S believes that it is false that p, and
  (ii) in saying to A that p S intends to deceive S about whether p.

Thus we have five different analyses of lying in four short chapters of Augustine's treatise. Which one is correct? Is one correct?

Astonishingly, Augustine does not decide. Here is his final judgment:

> T11. One may doubt whether a lie is told when someone does not desire to deceive; or when someone acts so that his hearer may not be deceived, although he wishes to make a false statement because in that way he will convince the other of the truth; or likewise, whether a lie is told when someone deliberately tells the truth in order to deceive another. However, *no one doubts that he lies who deliberately says what is false with the intention of deceiving* [emphasis mine]. It is clear, then, that a lie is a false statement made with the desire to deceive. But, whether this alone is a lie is another question. (4.5)

In a remarkable conclusion to a remarkable consideration of possible cases of lying, Augustine concludes that the three conditions of the Standard Analysis give us at least *sufficient conditions* for telling a lie. But he seems unwilling to maintain that all three conditions must be met for there to be a lie.

Although, as I mentioned at the beginning of this chapter, Augustine does go on to write a second treatise on lying, he never provides what he considers a satisfactory analysis of what it is to tell a lie. I also mentioned at the beginning that Augustine was dissatisfied with *On Lying*, although, in the end, he allowed it to be counted as one of his works. Perhaps he was dissatisfied with it because he was not able to settle on the correct analysis.

I suggest that this treatise is like one of Plato's aporetic dialogues – those called "aporetic" because they end in *aporia*, that is, in perplexity. I suggest further that it is a mark of Augustine's philosophical integrity that he allowed this work to stand as testimony to how problematic he found the notion of telling a lie to be.

further reading
William E. Mann, "To catch a heretic: Augustine on lying," *Faith and Philosophy* 20 (2003): 479–95. This article is a more nearly comprehensive consideration of what Augustine says about lying.

happiness

Near the end of *The City of God*, Augustine states simply and without qualification, "There is no reason for a human being to do philosophy except to be happy" (19.1). One might think that Augustine meant by these words that doing philosophy is great fun, and that having fun is what makes doing philosophy rewarding. Some of the philosophical passages in Augustine do suggest that he found puzzling over philosophical conundra a source of real pleasure. But some of the time he clearly found doing philosophy hard work, even uncongenial work. In any case, what he meant in this passage, I am quite sure, is that the only real justification for doing philosophy is the pursuit of the supreme good, and what makes the attainment of the supreme good attractive is the prospect it offers of making us happy.

Philosophers today might find it a little embarrassing to give expression to such a grand sentiment. Still, finding this sentiment expressed so prominently in Augustine should at least make clear how important happiness was to his conception of doing philosophy. Although we philosophers may now look for less grand ways to talk about the pursuit of happiness, as well as less grandiose ways to justify spending our time doing philosophy, we should find thinking about happiness no less important to philosophy than Augustine did, and the difficulties in being clear about what it is, or might be, and how it can be achieved, no less daunting.

In fact, Augustine thought and wrote about happiness throughout his long and prolific career. Book 1 of his earliest surviving work, *Against the Academicians*, takes up the relation between truth and happiness. Indeed, even before he had finished writing that work, Augustine turned out a little treatise specifically devoted to happiness, *The Happy Life* (*De beata vita*). His continuing preoccupation with the topic of happiness is reflected in most of his major works, including his *Confessions*, *On the Trinity*, and *The City of God*.

It is certainly not surprising to find that such a restless and probing thinker might change his mind somewhat about happiness over his incredibly prolific lifetime. Yet in addition to changes of mind there are also striking continuities, very striking continuities. I shall make no attempt here to trace the various developments in Augustine's thinking on the subject of happiness, interesting though they be. Instead I shall focus on an important contrast between two concepts of happiness to be found in his thought. Although, as I shall point out along the way, each of these two concepts finds expression in several of Augustine's works, I shall concentrate on two especially rich discussions of happiness to bring out the nature and importance of these two concepts.

The first of the two concepts, what I shall call the "Experiential Concept of Happiness," I find developed in Book 10 of Augustine's *Confessions*. The second, what I shall call the "Formal Concept of Happiness," is perhaps best presented in Book 13 of his treatise *On the Trinity*. Let us turn, then, first to Confessions 10 and the Experiential Concept of Happiness.

Book 10 of the *Confessions* is a discussion of memory (*memoria*). Augustine uses the term 'memory' very broadly in this book, more broadly, I think, than anywhere else in his writings. To be sure, Augustine has a special interest here in what we, too, would call "memory." But the claims he makes about memory in this book come close enough to what Augustine later says about mind (*mens*) in Book 10 of *The Trinity* that we might almost translate *memoria* in this book as 'mind.'

As for happiness, Augustine begins his discussion of it in Chapter 20 of Book 10, where he announces that in looking for God he is looking for happiness, that is, "the happy life" (*beata vita*). "But how then," he asks in puzzlement, "can I search for that?" The worrying idea seems to be that to have happiness in one's mind, one would need actually to be happy, or at the very least, to have been happy. There is even the suggestion that, in order to have a fully clear and satisfactory conception of happiness, one would need to be, or to have been at some time, completely happy. Perhaps you can already understand why I have chosen to call the concept of happiness that emerges from this discussion, the "Experiential Concept." Knowing what happiness is is knowing the experience of being happy.

Augustine's inclination to say that only someone who has experienced happiness can know what it is persists throughout Book 10 of the *Confessions*. It should not be dismissed as a simple mistake. It is connected to a deep worry about how things can be in the mind at all, that is, in memory. Here is one of many passages in which Augustine reflects with puzzlement and perplexity on the grandeur, but also on the limitations, of the mind, and what we can find in it.

T1. This power of memory is great, great beyond measure, O God. It is a vast and boundless sanctuary. Who can plumb its depths? And yet this is a power of my mind [*animus*]. It is part of my nature, and I myself do not take in all that I am. Therefore the mind [*animus*] is too narrow to contain itself. But where is that part of it which it does not itself contain? Is it somewhere outside itself and not within it? How then can it be part of it, if it is not contained in it? (10.8.15)

Augustine thinks of the mind as receiving messages through the senses. So things may be present to my mind, my memory, by my seeing or hearing or otherwise perceiving them. They may also be present to my mind by my having an image (*imago*), or likeness (*similitudo*), of them. Finally, he thinks that what we today might want to call abstract objects, such as numbers, can be present to memory directly, without any representation at all.

In whatever way happiness, or the happy life, is in my mind, it may seem that I should have to be, or to have been, happy to know what happiness is. Certainly if it is present nonrepresentationally, the way numbers are, what is there would have to be "the real thing." If it were present only representationally, the mental image would have to be, it seems, a *similitudo*, a likeness. And the likeness of happiness would, of course, have to be something that resembles happiness. So to think about what happiness is I must either get happiness itself into my mind, or at least have something there very much like it.

Augustine tries to drive his point home by drawing a contrast between happiness and eloquence.

> T2. In hearing this word ['eloquence'] even people who are not yet eloquent themselves, though they would like to be, recall the thing itself. From this it is clear that they already have knowledge of it. By means of the bodily senses they have observed eloquence in others. It has given them pleasure and they too want to be eloquent . . . [By contrast] there is no bodily sense by which we can experience happiness [*beata vita*] in others. (10.21.30)

And so happiness could not get into my memory by perception, through the bodily senses, of other people who are happy.

So how did happiness get into my memory so that I can think about it and know what it is? Perhaps it is there, Augustine suggests, the way remembered *pleasures* are there. He continues:

> T3. Even when I am sad I can recall pleasure [*gaudium*],[1] just as I can recall happiness [*beata vita*] when I am miserable. Yet I have never, by any of the bodily senses, either seen or heard or smelled or tasted or touched the pleasure I have. But it is something I have experienced in my mind when I have been glad, and the knowledge of it has remained firmly in my memory, so

that I can always recall it, sometimes with disgust and sometimes with longing, according to the differences between the things which I remember having taken pleasure in. (10.21.31)

In fact, the move from happiness to mere *pleasure* actually raises another philosophical problem for Augustine. He thinks that the possibility of remembering pleasure when one is sad is profoundly puzzling. Suppose that what I have in my *memoria* when I think about what pleasure is, or recall a bit of pleasure I have had, is a bit of pleasure itself. But if that were right, then merely thinking about the pleasure should displace the sadness. Of course it might do that, but it need not. It might make me even sadder at my present state, or more resentful, or just nostalgic, to think about pleasure, especially, perhaps, a pleasure I have had in the past.

Alternatively, suppose that the pleasure I have in my memory when I think about what pleasure is, or recall a moment of pleasure from my past, is only a likeness. It is not clear that this alternative is any less puzzling. To do its job, a likeness of pleasure would have to be like pleasure in a relevant respect. And what could that relevant respect be if it were not something that made the likeness pleasurable to entertain? Again, just thinking about what pleasure is, or remembering a past pleasure, should therefore be pleasurable. Yet, clearly, it need not be pleasurable at all.

So far as I can see, Augustine never resolves this problem to his own satisfaction. It offers a basis for criticizing the idea that there must be mental images of feelings and emotional states in the mind for us to be able to think about these feelings and emotional states.

Suppose now it is not just a momentary pleasure that is in my mind, but happiness itself, what Augustine often calls "the happy life" [*beata vita*]. "Where and when, then," Augustine asks, "did I experience my happiness [*beata vita*] so that I am able to remember it and love it and long for it?" He continues:

> T4. I am not alone in this desire, nor are there only a few who share it with me. Absolutely everyone wants to be happy. Unless we knew happiness with a firm knowledge [*certa notitia*], we would not want it with such a firm desire. But what is this [happiness we so firmly desire]? What [is it]? (10.21.31)

In these few words Augustine makes a number of claims and assumptions that I want to isolate and focus on in this chapter. Most obviously there is a claim that the desire for happiness is universal. Thus:

(1) Everyone wants to be happy.

Augustine asserts in many places that the desire for happiness is universal. It is not, of course, an original claim with him. But, as we shall see, it makes trouble for some of the other things Augustine wants to say about human happiness.

Quite plausibly, Augustine thinks that, since everyone wants to be happy, everyone must know what happiness is. In fact, Augustine actually says everyone knows what it is with a firm knowledge. Dropping the intensification, we can say that Augustine thinks that accepting the claim that everyone wants to be happy commits him at least to this:

(2) Everyone knows what happiness is.

As I have already made clear, Augustine thinks that knowing what happiness is requires that one either be currently happy or at least have had the experience of being happy. That idea is also alluded to at the beginning of the quotation above. So he is also committed to this experiential requirement for knowledge:

(3) No one knows what happiness is who has not had the experience of being happy.

Realizing that everyone wants to be happy and everyone knows what happiness is, might well lead us to expect, contrary to our life experience, that people would all make similar choices in life. Augustine gives this example:

> T5. If two people were asked whether they wanted to be soldiers, it could be that one of them would say he wanted to and the other not. If, however, it were asked of them whether they wanted to be happy [*beati*], without hesitation they would both immediately say they wanted that. Nor would it be on account of anything other than to be happy [*beati*] that this one would want to be a soldier and that one not. Unless, perhaps, one person takes pleasure [*gaudet*] from this and the other one from that? In this way everyone agrees on wanting to be happy in the way they would agree, if they were asked, on wanting to be pleased [*gaudere*]. And, in fact, they call this very pleasure [*gaudium*] happiness [*beata vita*]. (10.21.31)

Augustine could have used the soldiering choice to make the point that, whereas some people suppose it is pleasure that makes one happy, others suppose that it is honor, specifically, the honor of fighting in battle. Instead, he treats the volunteer soldier as agreeing to join the army because he anticipates having pleasure in soldiering, whereas the refusenik anticipates that he would find little or no pleasure in a military life. So far, then, Augustine seems to think 'happiness' means 'having pleasure.'

He can allow that one person may find pleasure in x and no pleasure in y, whereas another person may find pleasure in y and none in x.

So long as having pleasure is really what happiness is, there seems to be no conflict between accepting both (1), the thesis that everyone wants to be happy, and (2), the thesis that everyone knows what happiness is, and also accepting this truism:

(4) Different people have different aims in life.

Everyone can want to be happy and also know that happiness is having pleasure, yet one person can want to join the army and the other not because the first person expects to find the military life pleasurable and the second one does not.

Augustine concludes the chapter this way:

> T6. And, in fact, they call this very pleasure [*gaudium*] happiness [*beata vita*]. Although one person achieves it from this, another person from that, there is, nevertheless, one thing everyone tries to attain: having pleasure [*gaudeat*]. Because this thing [namely, pleasure] is something no one can say he has not experienced, it is thus found in memory and recognized when the word 'happiness' [*beata vita*] is heard. (10.21.31)

So, perhaps, happiness is just pleasure, or the having of it. Thus:

(5) Happiness is just pleasure [*gaudium*].

This thesis, (5), the "pleasure thesis," does offer a way to make the experience requirement for knowledge plausible. If happiness is just having pleasure, then, provided everyone has at one time experienced some pleasure, everyone has the basis for knowing what happiness is. This may seem much more promising than the suggestion Augustine had floated back in Chapter 20. If we all have a memory of happiness, he writes there, we must already have been happy [*beati*] before – "whether all of us one by one [*singillatim*] or in that man [namely, Adam] who first sinned." Although Augustine never rules out the possibility that we have a racial memory of Adam's paradisal happiness, the idea of making a memory of an ordinary past pleasure the vehicle for thinking about happiness *simpliciter* is clearly a more plausible option.

Still, attractive as the pleasure thesis is as a way of rendering plausible the commitment to (1), the thesis that everyone wants to be happy, and (2), the thesis that everyone knows what happiness is, Augustine soon rejects it. In Chapter 22 he introduces what we might think of as the Platonic distinction between true and false pleasures. Not surprisingly, it is only true pleasures, he thinks, that constitute happiness. "Happiness," he says, addressing God, "is to take pleasure in you and for you and because of you." This pleasure, he insists, is not available to infidels. The pleasure they pursue, he insists, is not true pleasure.

With this move Augustine rejects the pleasure thesis, or at least amends it to yield this:

(6) Pleasure in God, and only that, is happiness.

Assuming, as seems beyond dispute, that not everyone knows that only pleasure in God is happiness, accepting (6) amounts to a denial of (2), the claim that everyone knows what happiness is, and therefore also (1), the claim that everyone wants to be happy. Augustine is entirely clear about this. He begins Chapter 23 with the admission "It is therefore not certain that everyone wants to be happy, because those who do not take pleasure in you [O God], which is the only happiness, do not want happiness in any case."

Augustine makes a game effort to salvage the plausibility of (1) by appealing to the idea that God is Truth and everybody wants the truth. People do like to deceive others, he admits; but, he insists, nobody likes to *be* deceived. And so, in this way, everyone wants to be happy.

Whatever other reasons there might be for saying that only pleasure in God constitutes real happiness, Augustine's effort to salvage (1), the thesis that everyone wants to be happy, seems to be a failure. Even if it were true that nobody likes to be deceived, and even if this fact were enough to justify a claim that everyone wants the truth, it is wildly implausible to think that everyone knows happiness to be taking pleasure in the truth. And so, if happiness were pleasure in the Truth, and only that, it would remain implausible to say that everyone wants to be happy.

* * *

Before I go on to the next key text and to the second concept of happiness in Augustine, let me reflect a bit on what has happened in these middle chapters of *Confessions* 10. Augustine seems there to be firmly committed to the thesis that everyone wants to be happy. He wards off the threat to the thesis that everyone wants to be happy posed by the obvious fact that people pursue strikingly different aims in life by pointing out that what gives pleasure to one person may give no pleasure to another. But then he dooms his analysis by adding that only pleasure in God is true happiness and it becomes false to say that everyone knows what happiness is, and therefore also false to say that everyone wants to be happy.

I want to turn now to a much later effort to deal with some of these very same issues, this time in Book 13 of Augustine's *On the Trinity*. Already in Chapter 3 of that book Augustine gives expression to the thesis that everyone wants to be happy. Speaking of an imaginary character he has been describing, he writes:

T7. If he had said, "All of you want to be happy [*beati*] and you do not want to be miserable," he would have said something that no one would have failed to acknowledge in his own will. For whatever else it is that anyone secretly wills, he does not withdraw from this want which is sufficiently known to all and is in everyone. (13.3.6)

Clearly Augustine has not here retreated from the claim that everyone wants to be happy. But immediately following the quotation above, at the beginning of Chapter 4, Augustine turns his attention to (4), the thesis that different people have different aims in life. His concern is that the obvious diversity in aims that people pursue casts doubt on the assumption that everyone knows what happiness is, and therefore on the claim that everyone wants to be happy, plausible as that assumption may be. He writes:

T8. For if all knew it [i.e., happiness, *beatitudo*], it would not be considered by some to be in the goodness of soul, by others in the pleasure of the body, by others in both, by some in this thing, and by others in that thing. For as anything particularly pleased them, so they found in it the happy life. How, then, can all love so ardently what all do not know? (13.4.7)

He considers rejecting the claim that everyone wants to be happy:

T9. Shall we consider that to be false, therefore, which not even that Academician Cicero doubted (for the Academicians doubt everything), who, when he wanted to begin his argument in the dialogue *Hortensius* with something about which no one would doubt, said: "All of us certainly want to be happy." (13.4.7)

In the next chapter Augustine tries out the move, already familiar to us from his *Confessions*, of understanding happiness to be pleasure:

T10. Or can we perhaps escape from this awkward situation by recalling what we have previously stated, that everyone has considered happiness to be the things that most please them? (Epicurus, sensual enjoyment [*voluptas*]; Zeno, virtue; and someone else, some other thing.) So we may say that to live happily is nothing other than to live according to one's own pleasure [*delectatio*], and therefore, it is not false that all want to live happily, because all wish that which pleases [*delectat*] each. (13.5.8)

Taking his cue from Cicero, Augustine rejects this accommodation. If I take pleasure in getting something that is really bad for me, he reasons, then I am not made happy by taking pleasure in getting it.

So the pleasure thesis is again rejected. But this time Augustine does not move to the restriction that happiness-making pleasures are those, and only those, which are pleasures *in God*. Instead he moves to a Formal Concept of Happiness that gives him some hope of holding onto the pair of claims that (1) everyone wants to be happy and (2) everyone knows what happiness is. Here is where he makes this new move:

> T11. Therefore, since it is true that everyone wants to be happy, and all want this one thing with the most ardent love, and on account of it want other things, whatever they may be, and since no one can love that of which he is totally ignorant, what it is and what kind, nor can he be ignorant of what it is that he knows that he wants, it follows that all know happiness [*beata vita*]. But all who are happy have what they want, although not all who have what they want are at once happy. But they are at once miserable who either do not have what they want or who have what they do not *rightly* want [emphasis mine]. Therefore, he alone is happy who has all that he wants and wants nothing wrongly. (13.5.8)

In place of the pleasure-in-God thesis, then, we have this, which expresses his Formal Conception of Happiness:

(7) Happiness is wanting only what is good for you to get and then getting everything you want.

I doubt that many people, unprompted, would come up with (7) as their understanding of what happiness is. On the other hand, it is not wildly implausible that most people, after careful consideration of the available alternatives, would agree to something like it as their conception of what happiness is. If so, Augustine has come much closer to his objective of holding onto those favored theses than we might have expected.

One might have thought that the Formal Concept of Happiness we find in *On the Trinity* 13 is something Augustine arrived at by finding unsatisfactory his efforts to develop the Experiential Concept of Happiness in Confessions 10. This is not, however, the case. Consider this passage from his treatise *On the Practices of the Catholic Church*:

> T12. We all certainly want to live happily [*beate vivere*]. There is no one in the human race who would not assent to this sentence, almost before it is spoken. However, in my judgment "happy" cannot be said of one who does not have what he loves, whatever it may be; or of one who has what he loves, if it be hurtful; or of one who does not love what he has, even if it be the best. For one who desires what he cannot have is tortured; and one who obtains what is not to be desired is deceived; and one who does not desire what should be gotten is ill. Now in all these cases the mind [*animus*] cannot but be miserable, and misery and happiness [*beatitudo*] cannot reside

at the same time in one person; no none of these people would be happy. There remains a fourth case, as I see it, where the happy life can be found: when that which is best for a human being is both loved and had. For what else do we say is to be enjoyed [*frui*] except to have at hand what you love? Nor is anyone happy who does not enjoy that which is best for human beings. Nor is there anyone who enjoys this who is not happy. We must have at hand, then, what is best for us if we are to think of living happily [*beate vivere*]. (1.3.4)

This passage seems to have been written in the year 388, roughly a decade before the *Confessions* and three decades or so before Book 13 of *On the Trinity*. Yet it seems to contain all the elements of the Formal Concept of Happiness as elaborated and defended three decades later, plus a suggestion of the importance of enjoying [*fruor*] what is best for a human being. A few chapters later, at 1.11.18, Augustine says that to reach God is happiness. But the reason he can say that that is happiness is that he supposes reaching God is actually what is *best* for a human being. So even the infidel can want to be happy, and know what happiness is (i.e., wanting and getting what is best for a human being), although, in Augustine's judgment, the infidel can never actually be happy without ceasing to be what he is, namely, an infidel.

The puzzle is then this. Why, if Augustine had already thought out the Formal Concept of Happiness in 388, does he try to develop the Experiential Concept of Happiness in his *Confessions* some nine or ten years later, especially when that attempt seems so clearly doomed to failure?

Perhaps the answer is this. The Formal Concept of Happiness seems to leave open the possibility that, even though I had never experienced a moment of happiness, I could nevertheless understand perfectly well what happiness is, even what a paradisal life of complete happiness would be. I would need to know what a desire is, and what it is to have a desire satisfied. And I would have to have the idea that having certain of my desires satisfied would be good for me, whereas having others satisfied would not be. If I had those ideas, I could put them together and form the complex idea of having all my wants satisfied in a situation in which all and only things that it would be good for me to get were also things that I wanted. I would then have the Formal Concept of Happiness. And if that concept were a correct concept, I would know what happiness is. Surely I might still have no idea at all what it would be *like* to be happy, even for a moment. My suggestion is that Augustine in Book 10 of the *Confessions* wanted an account of happiness which would make clear how we could know what happiness is *like*, even what living a completely happy life would be *like*.

Why might it be interesting or important to have a concept of what it would be like to be happy, even completely happy? The answer, I think, is that having an experiential concept of happiness might help motivate one to do whatever it takes to become happy, whereas having only a formal concept would be much less likely to move the will to do what it takes to try to gain happiness.

It would not be surprising if Augustine had such a motivational aim in mind when he wrote *Confessions* 10. After all, Book 10 comes just after Book 9, near the end of which Augustine describes a beatifical vision he had with his mother, Monica, just days before she died. After giving us a very moving, heavily metaphorical, account of that mystical vision, Augustine asks us to suppose that this state "were to continue and all other visions of inferior things were to be withdrawn and this single vision were to ravish and absorb and envelope its beholder in inward pleasures [*interiora gaudia*] in such a way that for him life was eternally the same as that instant of understanding for which he had longed so much" (10.10.25). Augustine takes this beatific state to be announced by the words of Jesus "Come and enter into the joy [or pleasure, *gaudium*] of your Lord" (Matthew 25:21).

As Augustine tells the story in his *Confessions*, Monica then says that she is ready to die, having accomplished what she had set out to do, and that she has no more interest in earthly happiness (*felicitas terrena*). Five days later she develops a fever and soon dies. Having himself also had this vision of true happiness, Augustine, I am suggesting, wants to be able to say what it is *like* to be truly happy, in such a way that he could hold on to his assumption that everyone wants to be happy and so must also know what happiness is. Alas! His effort fails.

For purposes of comparison, we might note that Aristotle's conception of *eudaimonia* in the *Nicomachean Ethics* is also a formal concept (activity in accordance with virtue, and if there be several, in accordance with the best and most complete – in a complete life). Aristotle argues in Book 10 that the happiest life would be one of philosophical contemplation. He also argues that this life would be the most pleasant. But he does not try to give us a concept of what it would be *like* to lead such a life. Would it be like reexperiencing every day the thrill of proving Fermat's last theorem? If so, I might be able to extrapolate from the thrill of solving a cryptogram in the daily newspaper to what the ideal Aristotelian life of contemplation would be like. But Aristotle does not say. He does not even try to say. He just describes happiness formally by, for example, appeal to the idea of self-sufficiency. And certainly he does not consider an experiential concept of *eudaimonia* to be part of the *logos* of happiness. And that is a good thing too, since he, like Augustine, supposes that everyone wants to be happy and thus everyone must, in some way, already know what happiness is.

I shall not try to rate Augustine's Formal Concept of Happiness in comparison with the suggestion of Aristotle, or that of any other philosophers.

I rest happy with the conclusion that his effort to say what happiness is in this formal way is much more successful than his effort to provide an experiential concept. But I suggest that Augustine's failure to give a satisfactory experiential account of what happiness is *like* is just as important for us to reflect on as his relative success in giving a formal account of happiness.

In any case, it is, I think, entirely fitting that the first important philosopher in our Western tradition to try to do philosophy from a first-person point of view should have made the effort to say what it is like to be happy. If he had succeeded, he would have done all a philosopher can do to make us want all and only those things it would be good for us to get.

further reading

Bonnie Kent, "Augustine's ethics," in Eleonore Stump and Norman Kretzmann (eds.), *The Cambridge Companion to Augustine*. Cambridge: Cambridge University Press, 2001, pp. 205–33. Kent sets her discussion of happiness in Augustine within the context of his ethics.

note

1 *Gaudium* in Augustine is often translated 'joy.' A translator may choose 'joy' because it sounds more edifying than 'pleasure,' which I use here. Or the translator may fear that using 'pleasure' will make Augustine sound too much like a British empiricist. In fact, I have the opposite concern. I worry that 'joy' may sound pious and not robustly experiential. When Augustine writes here that *gaudium* is something he has experienced (*expertus sum*) in his mind when he has been glad (*quando laetatus sum*), I think he means to identify something quite robustly experiential.

index